THE DEVIL'S LABYRINTH

THE DEVIL'S LABYRINTH

Encounters with the Arctic

CLIVE JOHNSON

SWAN·HILL
PRESS

By the same author
Land of the Ice King

919.804
J665d
1995

Copyright © 1995 by Clive Johnson

First Published in the UK in 1995
by Swan Hill Press, an imprint of Airlife Publishing Ltd

British Library Cataloguing in Publication Data
  A catalogue record for this book
  is available from the British Library

ISBN 1 85310 211 3

Typeset by Hewer Text Composition Services, Edinburgh
Printed in England by St Edmundsbury Press Ltd.,
Bury St Edmunds, Suffolk

Swan Hill Press
an imprint of Airlife Publishing Ltd
101 Longden Road, Shrewsbury SY3 9EB

To Tracey and Hannah

The hull of the *'Fram'* being launched.

CONTENTS

The *Fram* beset in the Polar drift ice. The deck mounted windmill which was used to generate electricity, can clearly be seen.

INTRODUCTION

The North Pole means many different things to many different people. To some, it means the entire frozen wilderness perched on top of the world, which provides a home for polar bears, seals and, sadly to a much lesser degree in recent years, Eskimo hunters. To others, it has become a place of work, whether it be as a scientist working from a drifting polar station, or an oil worker on a rig off the north Alaskan coast. However, to a small but increasing number of individuals, the North Pole represents a strong personal challenge, as demanding and dangerous as it has always been. To these people, the North Pole means only one thing, and that is the deep and sometimes overwhelming desire to travel to that very precise mathematical point on the Earth's surface, where the days and nights are six months long, it is every day of the week all the time, and only one compass direction exists – south.

To reach this spot at the top of the world and to stand there with the Earth slowly rotating beneath your feet, has been a challenge for thousands of years. Countless expeditions over the years slowly nibbled away the degrees of latitude, until one day after many years of struggle and defeat, a bearded, fur-clad figure aimed his sextant at the sun. The sun sight was taken and a calculation made, revealing a position of 89°57′ north, only three nautical miles from man's goal through the centuries. If he stood on top of an ice ridge, the Pole would be in sight, but what would he see? Nothing. No land-mark, no land, just more and more of the same chaotic drifting ice, over which he had been struggling for many weeks.

To stand at exactly 90° north is almost impossible. The British polar explorer Wally Herbert described it as 'trying to stand on the shadow of a bird flying overhead'. This is all due to the fact that the surface on which you are travelling is made up of floating pans of ice, which are continually moving.

Of course, today it is possible to charter an aircraft and fly in reasonable comfort and safety to the Pole, take a photograph and return for supper. Indeed, this has now become a strong attraction to quite wealthy 'extreme tourists', and flights are now scheduled each spring. However, to accomplish this only requires a large bank balance and very little effort.

The fact that Everest has already been climbed doesn't make the mountain any easier to climb, and the same can be said for a journey across the Arctic drift ice to the North Pole. The risks and objective dangers are still just as deadly as they have always been. Also, if you think of the Pole in the same terms as the summit of a mountain, having reached that summit, you would not expect an aircraft waiting there to whisk you back to your base camp.

The way individuals choose to carry out their expeditions is personal to them. Some purposely set out with only just enough supplies to enable them to reach the Pole, which then places them in a rescue situation, requiring the use of air support to remove the expedition from the ice. This type of expedition can only be classed as supported.

Peary had four attempts at reaching the Pole before he finally succeeded, losing eight of his toes. I have failed twice, but still have all my toes. The reasons for the failures are a complex combination of conditions, equipment failure and sheer bad luck. Having said that, I am happy at the way I approached the problem and gained much personal satisfaction out of pitting my strength and skills against this labyrinth of ice and snow which only the Devil himself could have created. To even start to contemplate hauling heavily loaded sledges across the Arctic drift ice day after endless day, in temperatures which freeze all exposed flesh instantly, you have to be something like the Minotaur, half bull, half man . . . and half mad.

Clive Johnson

ALONE IN
THE LABYRINTH

'Crossing the threshold of the kingdom of cold'

Pain – all I could feel was the mind-numbing pain as life started to ooze back into my hard frozen feet. I allowed myself the pleasure of crying out when the pain was almost unbearable as no one could hear me. I was alone. No one could witness the tears as they trickled down my face and froze on to my beard. I was alone.

For what seemed like an eternity, I had been lying on my back holding my feet up as far as I could into the apex of my small one-man tent, hoping to absorb as much heat as possible into my frozen feet. With my small paraffin Primus stove pumped up almost to the point of exploding, it had taken an hour to thaw out and untie the laces of my boots, which when finally removed had revealed two hard, frozen and by now severely frostbitten feet. At −60°C the heat from my stove, even at full power, seemed to be instantly sucked away into the frozen atmosphere inside my tent. I spent the rest of the day in agony, slowly thawing out my frozen feet and cursing my bad luck. Time seemed to slow down, giving me plenty of time to assess my position. Sometimes I would convince myself that the frostbite injury wasn't really that bad and maybe, just maybe, it would very quickly recover allowing me to carry on. I knew from my previous polar experience that the frost injury to my feet was of such seriousness that it would almost certainly mean the end of my planned unsupported solo trek across the Arctic ocean to the North Pole. I continued to curse

11

my luck, and that such a thing could bring a sudden and final end to what had taken almost two years of my life to organise.

Five days earlier, I had been dropped off on the northern side of Ward Hunt Island in the far north of the Canadian North West Territories by a chartered Twin Otter aircraft, and had set out alone across the polar drift ice in an attempt to become the first person to reach the North Pole solo and unsupported. I was hauling enough food and fuel on my small sledge to survive for forty-five days. By my fourth day out from the coast, I caught up with a three-man American supported expedition, who had already been on the ice for eleven days. One of the expedition members had had enough and had been flown back to Resolute Bay, and the remaining two were finding the going very hard indeed.

As I approached the American camp, the two men came out to greet me. At first I could not say anything to them, as my lips were so numb with cold. One of the men then handed me a cup containing a little hot water, which I used to thaw out my mouth. I think that they were a bit surprised at the speed with which I had caught up with them. They had had an air-drop of supplies that morning and were intending to try and haul a few miles further north that afternoon. I had had a good haul and needed to eat, so pitched my tent while the American expedition packed up and headed north. I was in good spirits that evening as I cooked up my evening meal, but things were about to change. Throughout that evening the ice noise increased to almost deafening levels. All around the ice was in motion and I could hear the sound of rushing water underneath. This was my first experience of travel on the Arctic drift ice, so I had to accept it as normal and tried to sleep through it. At around three in the morning, all hell let loose outside. There was an almighty bang, followed by several other similar bangs, each one sending violent judders through the ice floe on which I was camped. Ice pressure had been building up all day and I suppose something had to give sooner or later, but it was just my luck that what appeared to be giving was the bit of ice upon which I had chosen to sleep! My floe was about quarter of a mile in diameter and made up of quite thick multi-year drift ice which made it stand higher out of the water than the surrounding ice.

Day five dawned clear and cold, but outside the icescape had changed dramatically. To the west, a large pressure ridge had formed to a height of about twenty feet, and to the south a large pressure ridge over which I had struggled yesterday had now disappeared. Some distance to the north, I could see a foggy grey plume of frost smoke indicating the presence of open water, and my thermometer read −55°C. As I packed my sledge and hauled away to the north from my camp site, I had little idea just what a nasty shock Fate had got in store for me, and it was just as well.

That evening I tuned in the small lightweight high-frequency radio and listened for the scheduled call from my friend Ben Wallace-Hadrill, who had stationed himself at Resolute Bay some 800 miles to the south as my contact for the duration of the expedition. At the planned time a faint but readable voice could be heard through the atmospheric hum and crackle: 'British mobile, British mobile, British mobile, this is Resolute Bay, Resolute Bay, do you copy, over?' The sound of another human voice seemed almost unnatural as during the day I walked in complete silence, with only the sounds of the ice as it creaked, banged, bumped and groaned to keep me company. I spent the next few minutes relaying to Ben the details of how the night before the ice floe on which I was camped had split in half, opening up a lead of open water some five metres wide. With the night air temperature dropping to −65°C the lead had quickly frozen over with new ice about three centimetres thick, and by morning it was covered with beautiful frost flowers. Ice pressure was building up and the entire area was very active. The noise at times was deafening as the ice floes broke up under the relentless unseen pressure. I had tested the new ice with my usual test of 'if it can stand two blows from my ice axe without water bubbling up then it is strong enough to take my weight'. It passed the ice axe test OK, so I stepped out on to the ice. In order to pull my sledge to the edge of the ice floe I stepped close to the edge of the lead. Here the ice was much thinner, and without warning it opened up and I sank up to my waist in inky black water. With my ice axe still in my hand I was quickly able to haul myself out on to the thicker ice and back to the safety of the floe. Both of my boots had filled with water which almost instantly froze solid around my feet. My clothing also froze, but that was the least of my problems. I had to get back to a safe area, put up my tent, get the stove going, thaw out and remove my boots as quickly as possible. By the time I had put up my tent, all feeling in my feet had disappeared, the water in my boots was now frozen solid, and I knew I was in trouble.

Ben, as always, was calm and professional on the radio, but was obviously anxious to know what my plan of action would be from now on. After further discussion, we agreed that the best plan would be to carry on as normal and see to what degree the frost damage developed over the next day or so and then make a decision. One more day's march was enough to tell me that it was all over. It was quite obvious that I would have to return to civilisation for medical treatment to my feet or risk losing some of my toes. Much worse than the pain of the frostbitten toes was the thought that I must also face the critics, of which I had many, all of whom said that an unsupported journey was impossible.

Twelve hours later the sound of aircraft engines filled my ears as the tiny Twin Otter aircraft appeared overhead. After several low passes, it made an approach to land about two hundred metres away on the far side of a very high pressure ridge. I stood and watched in amazement and horror as the pilot jockeyed the plane on to the right line before it disappeared behind the ridge. There was a roar of engines and the plane re-appeared and circled round to make another pass. This time the plane came in very low, and by the tone of the engines it seemed that the pilot had made the decision to land. Again the plane disappeared from sight behind the high pressure ridge, and within seconds I could hear the loud roar as the Twin Otter's engines went into reverse thrust. Just then I saw the tail plane of the Otter rise and fall above the crest of the ridge in a cloud of violently swirling spindrift.

All went quiet. I can remember thinking 'Well that's the end of that!' as I scrambled to the top of the ridge to take a look at what must now be a pile of smoking wreckage on the ice. To my astonishment, there in the middle of a mass of pressure ice stood the Otter, apparently none the worse even after such a rough landing. However, there was one small problem remaining: how were we going to take off?

Within minutes all my gear had been loaded on to the aircraft and I stood with the pilot and looked at the possibilities for a take-off run. I asked him, 'How the hell do you plan to take off from this place?' He looked at me and gave a confident 'Well', you see that first hump over there? By the time we hit that I don't think we will have enough speed to take off. I looked at him and said, 'Then what?' Again he started with a long drawn out 'Well, we'll be knocked into the air by that all right, but we'll come straight down again.' He then pointed to a second hump of ice a little way beyond the first and said, 'But you see that second hump? Well, I reckon that by the time that one knocks us into the air we might just have enough speed to stay up and clear the pressure ridge. Then I'm heading south.' I started to say 'What if . . .' but the pilot stopped me in mid-question saying 'Right, well, we'd better be going.' I can remember thinking that it would have been a silly question anyway, as we had no choice.

Ben had come on the flight along with Philip Jordan and Steve Bent, a reporter and photographer respectively from the *Mail on Sunday* who were following my expedition. I could see that our newspapermen were a bit apprehensive about the situation, but Ben didn't seem bothered at all; in fact I think he totally enjoyed the adventure.

Soon the aircraft was taxied over to one side of the floe as close to the edge as possible, then swung around to face the desired direction. The surface was so uneven that while taxying the plane rocked from side to side so much that the wing tips almost hit the ice. We waited for a few minutes as the pilot went through his preflight checks. Just before take-off the co-pilot popped his head through the door and said, 'This one's going to be close, so can you all move as far into the tail as you can before we start the take-off run and hold on tight.' The engines revved up to full power and at first nothing happened, but then the plane started to move slowly, wallowing across the uneven surface. It then picked up speed and began to rumble and clatter across the broken ice before we hit the first hump. As the pilot predicted the plane was tossed into the air but without sufficient speed to remain airborne, and we came crashing down again. I could not possibly see how the plane could pick up enough speed to take off before the second hump, and I prepared for the worst by gripping the cargo straps until my knuckles were white. The second hump arrived with a thud and the plane rose into the air. I held my breath and waited for that sinking feeling before the plane hit the ice once more, but it didn't arrive. We were airborne. The little plane clawed its way into the air against all odds and just managed to clear the high pressure ridge at the far side of the floe. The pilot turned around and looked at us with a look that said 'I bet you thought I couldn't do it'. Too bloody right! I looked around and there was a distinct look of relief on the faces of our *Mail on Sunday* men!

Back at Resolute Bay, I had my feet checked over at the local hospital. The nurse took one look at them and said, 'Jesus, you've done a real good number on them, you'll be lucky to save them. The usual treatment is . . .' She then made a chopping action with her hand. I thought that I would return home for a second opinion.

We had over a week to wait for our flight home, so we decided to make the most of it. Ben arranged for the loan of a couple of skidoos, a sledge and a two-man pyramid tent from a local outfitter. For the next five days, we sledged out from Resolute, across the sea ice to Bathhurst Island via little Cornwallis Island. Our route took us north along the east coast of Bathhurst Island to the area of the magnetic North Pole. During our journey, we saw lots of bear tracks, but never saw a single animal. Because of our proximity to the magnetic pole, our compasses were useless, which made navigation difficult. The islands in this region are low lying and they all look alike, especially at this time of year with their thick covering of winter snow.

Back home in England I faced the depression of failure, but had a strange feeling that Fate had been at work and, although ultimate success had been far from on the cards, I had been successful in initiating a new era in Arctic expeditions. The start of a new way of approaching expedition logistics. You can compare it with the developments in Himalayan climbing. In the past large teams of climbers used 'siege' tactics on mountains, laying thousands of feet of fixed ropes between numerous camps along the route in order to reach the summit. Advances made in the design of clothing and equipment, added to the increasing amount of knowledge relating to high-altitude physiology. This method has now become obsolete. Now it is common practice for small lightweight expeditions to make ascents of the highest peaks without any support teams or fixed ropes and camps. This same natural evolution was happening to polar expeditions, and in the Arctic things were about to change.

Can any North Pole expedition be completely 'unsupported'? I think not, as it all depends on the individual expedition's definition of the word. I would argue that it would be more correct to say that an expedition sets out to be as 'independent' as possible. For me, the reason I didn't plan to use air support was quite simple: I just could not afford it! Air charter is very expensive, and for two years I had searched for commercial sponsorship to fund my expedition. Eventually, in early 1985, I just scraped enough funds together to pay for a charter flight from Resolute Bay in Canada to Ward Hunt Island on the northern coast of Ellesmere Island, the closest point of land to the Pole itself. Many expeditions had set out from Ward Hunt Island, but all these expeditions had relied heavily on the use of air support to resupply them with food and fuel en route to the Pole. In theory, this method should always bring success, just as long as the expedition members can keep putting one foot in front of the other. To set out from the coast to the Pole in one push manhauling all the supplies you will require for the entire expedition on a lightweight sledge is a far more challenging proposition.

As the frostbite injury to my feet slowly recovered, I began to analyse the meaning of 'unsupported' in the context of expeditions and tried to bring the whole realm of adventure, exploration and human endeavour back into polar expeditions. To have 'support' as part of an expedition's logistics really means that the expedition is protected against failure. Should something go wrong then the 'support' puts it right, and the expedition continues to predictable success. When this kind of support is employed it removes a vital element from the expedition; in order to further its progress, it places a high reliance on outside technical assistance to attain its goal, and the balance between the adventurer and the unknown is completely destroyed by the 'attainment of the goal at all costs' attitude. I have always wanted to feel that I have earned my chances to reach the Pole, and to make the attempt with all due respect and humility. For me the polar regions, both North and South, are so elemental that in my opinion man should not have the right, or more to the point any need, to subdue its many challenges with technology. The Arctic is an environment so wild and untameable that it is more than capable of stopping even the best prepared and equipped expedition. This is the nub of the 'unsupported' debate. The Arctic ocean offers a supreme challenge to independent expeditions, but, when the use of air support is added to the plan, the challenge and subsequently the whole point of being there fades away to nothing. Obviously, I fully appreciate that expeditions which are carrying out extensive scientific programmes must be supported in any way suitable to facilitate the completion of the project. This is understandable and accepted, but for expeditions where adventure is the main objective, air support must only be thought of in an emergency situation.

Expeditions are extraordinary creatures: they don't just happen, they evolve. This evolutionary process starts with the minutest spark of an idea, which simmers for a while before heating up and eventually boiling over into a passionate frenzy of energy which nothing will be allowed to stop. Each member of the expedition becomes swamped under an ever-increasing amount of letter writing, telephone calls and meetings with sponsors and potential sponsors. If an expedition is organised, funded and gets under way within one year, this would be exceptional. The normal gestation period of an expedition is two to three years, and in some cases a lot longer. I remember a conversation with the Russian explorer Dmitry Shparo, who led in the first Russian expedition to the North Pole. He told me that they were first ready to leave in 1971, but due to government red tape and bureaucracy they had to wait seven years. During this period he had to keep the team enthusiasm alive, along with a continuous physical fitness programme.

In 1978, Dmitry Shparo and his team had set out for the Pole from Henrietta Island, which is the most northerly island in the New Siberian group of islands, situated off the northern coast of Siberia, with the full backing and support of the Russian government. The expedition relied on three pre-planned resupply air drops en route to the Pole, and, not unpredictably, seventy-six days after leaving Henrietta Island, Shparo and his team reached the North Pole. To mount the same heavily supported expedition today would be far too expensive, so much so that it would be very hard indeed to justify the expense. Having support aircraft resupply an expedition en route totally destroys the adventure element of the project, where the team must overcome any problems through skill and resourcefulness. When problems pile up and become insurmountable then the expedition has reached its end. To have aircraft standing by, ready to replace food, fuel, equipment and personnel etc., as and when needed, just makes the eventual attainment of the expedition's goal an unsatisfying, empty event.

The uncertain outcome common to all unsupported expeditions attracts a different type of traveller. These expeditions require meticulous planning and preparation. Another major problem is the mental and physical problems as you prepare for such a journey. Coming to terms with the enormity of the task which you have set for yourself calls for serious self-analysis. The objective dangers inherent in polar expeditions must be rationalised. Previous experience and knowledge gained over many years of polar expeditioning can help to reduce most objective dangers to a reasonably acceptable level.

Before embarking on any polar expedition, I feel it is important always to ask yourself this question: 'Will I enjoy being there?' If you have to sit and think about the answer, then don't go. I have often been asked 'Why do you do these expeditions?', and my reply is one which I heard a long time ago but which says it all: 'Some people feel the need to ask that question, others feel the answer so there is no need to ask the question.' It all comes down to personal enjoyment, the deep feeling of joy just to be there even though you are cold, tired, hungry and you are always wondering if your team mates are hurting more than you. Long after the expedition is over, you forget the bad days and the pain and remember the beauty and raw wildness, which then starts to draw you back over and over again. Peary called this strange attraction 'polar fever'.

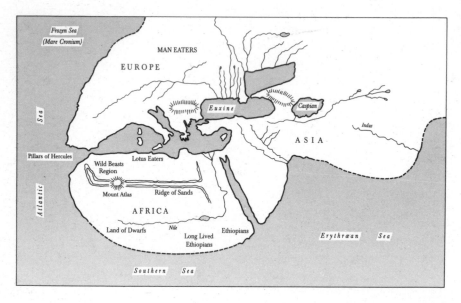

Map of the known world according to Herodotus in the fifth century B.C. It is interesting to note, that even at this time, they knew of a 'frozen sea' to the north.

BEYOND THULE

The first polar explorer

The ancient Greeks have a reputation for having produced some of history's greatest philosophers, mathematicians and astronomers, but it is now accepted that they also produced the first great polar explorer. His name was Pytheas.

Pytheas lived and worked in the Greek colonial city of Massilia (now Marseille) around the fourth century BC. Pytheas refused to take notice of all that was thought and taught about the world as known by the Greeks, that beyond the known populated regions there stretched out a dark region full of terrible sea monsters, floating sea grass and thick black waters which marked the edge of 'the void'. Pytheas knew that the earth was round and strongly suspected that the Carthaginian Himlico, who around a hundred years earlier had sailed north and returned with tales of sea monsters, had simply lied in order to discourage future competition.

In the days of Pytheas sea travel was very common indeed, and in the Mediterranean trade by merchant shipping was well established. However, their means of navigation was less advanced. The ancient Greek merchantmen would hug the coastline during the day, and before darkness fell they beached their boats and would then wait until daylight before they set sail once more. The simple compass had not yet been introduced to Europe, although it is thought that the Chinese had already invented it by 1200 BC. It was not until sometime in the twelfth century AD that the compass made its way via the Crusades from China to Christian Europe.

Knowledge of astronomy, mathematics and geography was the main aid to navigation available to Pytheas on sea voyages around the Mediterranean. Even as long ago as the fourth century BC, the standard practice of taking onboard a 'pilot' when approaching a foreign port was common. The pilot, whose name is derived from the Basque word 'pilotois' meaning 'magician', once onboard would take command of the vessel and using his wealth of local knowledge would work his magic by steering the vessel on a safe course into port.

The theory and techniques of navigation were a passion to Pytheas, a scientist and mathematician studying with Eudoxus, who was a student of Plato. It was Eudoxus who proved to Pytheas that the Earth was indeed round, and he was the first man to set the length of one year accurately at 365¼ days. Pytheas knew how to determine latitude by using the gnomon, which was the earliest astronomical instrument invented, but by whom is unknown. The gnomon is thought to have been used almost since the dawn of time by the peoples of many countries of the world. Basically, it is made from a tall pillar of stone several metres high which is marked off with a scale made up of 120 equal graduations. This same scale is then marked out on the ground radiating out from the base of the pillar. It was then a very simple but lengthy process of measuring the length of the shadow cast by the gnomon. By measuring the sun's shadow and taking careful notes over several months to include the longest and the shortest days of the year, Pytheas was able to calculate latitude. Although not very accurate, the gnomon remained in use for many centuries. It would have been out of the question for Pytheas to have used a gnomon onboard ship to determine his latitude, but it is known that Pytheas first discovered that the pole star (Polaris) was not precisely fixed above the Pole, thus not an exact indication of true north for navigation purposes. Observations of the stars could not have been made using the gnomon, which would prompt one to wonder if Pytheas had some other instrument at his disposal, details of which remain a mystery.

'Latitude', in geographical terms, can be defined as the angular distance between any given point on the globe and the Equator, this angle being expressed in degrees. Pytheas knew that the Earth was a sphere, so he must have calculated that the highest possible latitude had to be 90°, both to the North and South Poles.

At the time of Pytheas, there was a strong belief in a theory which divided the Earth into five distinct zones: one totally uninhabitable because it was too near to the sun; two reasonably habitable because they lay a moderate distance from the sun; and two zones uninhabitable because they were too far from the sun. It was also thought that should the explorer penetrate beyond Europe, then he would find a paradise where the air was clear, golden fruit grew and one-legged people, the Unipeds, lived. The Unipeds are said to have had many strange qualities, such as never growing old; making way for the next generation was a simple matter of committing suicide at the right time!

You have to sympathise with Pytheas, surrounded by the many eminent Greek philosophers of the day, arguing that the earth was flat and strange people lived in the north lands and many other odd theories; he must have felt exasperated. His own scientific observations were telling him that all the contemporary theories were incorrect. It was little wonder that for long after his death the dominant philosophers of the time, and in particular the Greek geographer Strabo (c.63 BC – AD 20), went so far as to call Pytheas a liar.

Little is known about the personal status of Pytheas. For instance, his date of birth is not known for certain and his place of death is also unknown. Scant fragments of information suggest that he was not a wealthy man and Strabo, one of Pytheas's greatest detractors, wrote, 'it seems incredible for an individual possessing no means whatsoever to undertake on his own initiative an expedition of such far-reaching extent'. I would suggest that Pytheas, along with many of the great explorers throughout history, must have sought commercial support in order to finance his voyages. Commerce would fund his voyages and in return Pytheas would seek out new trading opportunities, from which his sponsors might increase their fortunes. It would also seem reasonable to assume that the town government of Massilia would also have given Pytheas their patronage and helped in some way to finance his voyage into the unknown.

Thus, at some time in the fourth century BC, Pytheas put together the first true polar expedition. His ship would probably have been a Greek trireme, with three tiers of oars and carrying around 200 oarsmen. Sir Clements Markham writes of such vessels:

> 'A large Massilian ship was a good sea-boat, and well able to make a voyage into the northern ocean. She would be from 150 to 170 feet long – the beam of a merchant ship being a quarter and of a warship one-eighth the length – with a depth of hold of twenty-five or twenty-six feet, and a draught of ten to twelve. Her tonnage would be 400 to 500, so that the ship of Pytheas was larger and more seaworthy than the crazy little *Santa Maria* with which, eighteen hundred years afterwards, Columbus discovered the New World.'

Sailing west through the Mediterranean, Pytheas reached the 'Pillars of Hercules' in the Straits of Gibraltar. It is not known if he came across hostile Carthaginians at this point, for it is known that they were keeping a permanent blockade in this area in order to protect their trade in tin and amber along the Atlantic coast. It is thought that Pytheas may have sneaked past the Carthaginians under the cover of darkness, using his skills in astronomical navigation to good effect.

When Pytheas eventually reached the Atlantic, he came across a strange and interesting phenomenon: tides. Pytheas was fascinated by this phenomenon and sought an explanation. This he achieved and thus became the first astronomer to establish a link between the attraction of the moon and tidal cycles. Once out into the north Atlantic, Pytheas was free to head north and explore the unknown. It is known that he sailed across the Bay of Biscay and through the English Channel to make his first landfall in Kent (Caesar's Cantium), although he could have landed at any point along the south coast of England and more than likely did, as he was also seeking new sources of tin for his commercial sponsors. From Kent he sailed north along the east coast of Britain to Flamborough Head and on north to the Orkney Islands, then known as 'Orkan'. It was almost certain that it was while Pytheas was in the Orkney Islands that he first heard tales of a strange and mysterious island which was said to be situated in the icy region somewhere to the north. The island was called Thule.

There are many claims to the origin of the word 'Thule'; some say it is derived from the Saxon words 'thyle' etc, all of which mean 'limit' or 'boundary'. To the barbarians of Britain, Thule could simply have been their word for 'the end of the world', or *Meta incognita* and not the name of an island at all. The famous Norwegian polar explorer Fridtjof Nansen in his writings adds a couple of Gothic words, 'tiele' and 'tiule', which also mean 'boundary'. Thule, which was later christened 'Ultima Thule', has been the source of much argument and debate over its position or whether it simply existed in the imaginations of early mapmakers. However, in the time of Pytheas, the existence of Thule must have seemed very real and there for the taking. If only he could find it. It is said that Pytheas struck north from the Orkney islands and after six days at sea sighted Thule. Forgetting all the arguments relating to the geographical position of Thule, Pytheas in his trireme or convoy of biremes and triremes, must have been the first known explorer to cross the Arctic Circle, as he speaks of the midnight sun which is a phenomenon only experienced north of the Arctic Circle. He also speaks of meeting floating pack ice, which could put him north of Iceland.

Vilhjalmur Stefansson, the great polar explorer, in his book *Ultima Thule*, examines in minute detail all three main schools of thought which form the debate on Pytheas and the discovery of Thule. Some hold that Thule is Iceland; others, including the Norwegian Fridtjof Nansen maintain that Thule must have been Norway; a third school of thought suggests that Thule was in fact Jan Mayen Island. Stefansson in his book would appear to favour the Iceland – Thule argument. I think that I am inclined to agree with Stefansson purely on the grounds of probabilities.

When Pytheas returned to Massilia after a voyage which had lasted several years, and which included circumnavigating Britain and making a journey into the Baltic sea in the search of more amber, he settled down to write up the account of his adventures. His book *On the Ocean* has been lost, leaving only quotations from other writers of the time and other small fragments of information with which to fuel the 'Thule' debate. One thing is certain: he was without doubt one of the greatest pioneer polar explorers. I think it would be naive of any polar historian to say that Pytheas was the 'first' polar explorer. He was almost certainly the first known polar explorer. However, it is not beyond the realms of possibility that there were, in history, many 'anonymous' explorers who made numerous exploratory journeys north of the Arctic Circle and who kept their findings secret. Who knows?

In the centuries after the death of Pytheas, the debate surrounding Thule continued. With Pytheas not around to defend himself, the jealous started a slow character assassination designed to discredit Pytheas forever. Two men in particular were the prime movers in the attempt to demolish the achievements of Pytheas: Polybius and Strabo. Being the geographical authorities of the era, Polybius and Strabo attacked Pytheas and made him out to be untrustworthy and mendacious. Thus a golden age of polar exploration began. Countless expeditions, with countless objectives and ulterior motives, set sail from numerous countries until at last only one major prize gripped the heart of every bearded, steady-eyed, square-jawed explorer worth his salt – the discovery and attainment of the Pole itself.

In 1755, an Act of Parliament was passed; this offered a reward of £5,000 for the first ship to sail within a degree of the Pole, and in 1773 Captain C. J. Phipps MP took two ships, the *Racehorse* and the *Carcass*, to sail directly to the Pole. It goes without saying that he did not succeed in reaching it. Phipps was stopped by the ice at 80°42'N just off Spitzbergen. The next high-latitude record breaker was the British whaling captain William Scoresby in 1806, when he reached latitude 81°30'N–19°E to the north of Spitzbergen. In 1818 the British Parliament, having lost all hope of anyone sailing to the North Pole, passed a new act which changed the objective to the discovery of a north-west passage as a new trade route. For this achievement they offered a reward of £20,000. This much larger reward money seemed to divert the attentions of all the British explorers to the north-west passage for many years, leaving the North Pole free for the taking. The most notable British expedition ever to set out to discover the north-west passage was led by a man called Sir John Franklin who, with Captain Francis Crozier in the *Terror* and *Erebus*, set out for the Arctic in 1845. After spending the winter on Beechey Island, the expedition pushed on until both ships became stuck in the ice near to King William Island and they were eventually abandoned in Victoria Sound. The tragic events which followed remain a mystery but took the lives of all 139 men on the expedition. Over the next ten years, some forty expeditions were sent in an attempt to find Franklin and his men. One of these search parties was led by Sir Edward Belcher. Belcher, it is said, had no Arctic experience; nevertheless, he was dispatched with four ships under his command. During the expedition Captain Leopold McClintock of HMS *Intrepid* made an impressive 1,408-mile independent manhauling journey, spending 105 days in the field. During the same expedition, Lieutenant Frederick Meecham sledged 1,336 miles in only 70 days!

The year 1827 saw the first serious attempt at reaching the Pole. Lieutenant Edward Parry in the *Hecla* put together an expedition the objective of which was to reach Treurenberg Bay in Spitzbergen, and from there he intended to drag 'sledge boats' over the drifting polar ice to the Pole. He didn't make it, but it was a tremendous effort. Parry and his men travelled over 900 miles across the drifting ice, but the strong drift and currents continuously pushed them back. They finally reached a new furthest north of 82°45'N at a point only 172 miles north of the ship. This record stood for forty-eight years.

In 1860, the American Isaac Hayes led an expedition in his ship the *United States* in an attempt to reach the North Pole via Smith Sound. Hayes was under the illusion that the Arctic ocean was free of ice, but he was soon trapped by it. Hayes then sledged across to Ellesmere Island and made a disputed claim of a furthest north of 81°35'N. This route of approach north via Smith Sound, later claimed by Peary to be 'the American route', was to be the scene of many heroic journeys and the key to the eventual discovery of the Pole.

Fifteen years after Hayes, George Nares and Henry Stephenson in HMS *Alert* and HMS *Discovery*, also under the illusion that you could sail across the Arctic ocean to the Pole, also tried to go by way of Smith Sound. The orders given to Nares from the Admiralty ran thus: 'Reach the highest northern latitude . . . if possible the North Pole!' The *Discovery* wintered at the north side of Lady Franklin Bay on Ellesmere Island and the *Alert* pushed on through Robeson Channel and set up winter quarters at Floeberg Beach. From the *Alert*, Albert Markham and Alfred Parr sledged to 83°20−N, breaking the record for the furthest north set by Parry in 1827. At the same time, Pelham Aldrich sledged west along the northern coast of Ellesmere Island as far as Yelverton Inlet, establishing Cape Aldrich and Cape Columbia as the most northerly points of Ellesmere Island at 82°06'N. Three men died during this expedition.

In year 1878 saw Baron Adolf Erik Nordenskjold, in an expedition sponsored by the Swedish government, successfully navigate the north-east passage, from west to east in the *Vega*, a sail and steam ship of only 300 tons. The ship was 150 feet long by twenty-nine feet wide, with one single screw propeller driven by a sixty-horsepower steam engine. With fuel and provisions for two years, the *Vega*, accompanied by three cargo ships which were to transport Siberian wheat back to Sweden, sailed north. On 27 September 1878 the ice stopped the *Vega* at 67°07'N, 173°31'E and she became icebound. During the harsh winter of this region, the ship's scientists made astronomical observations from an observatory made from snow, and made a study of the native Chukchi Indians. On 18 July 1879, the *Vega* broke free from the Arctic ocean's icy grasp and continued to break open a route to the east. Finally, at 11 a.m. on 20 July 1879, the *Vega* fired a five-gun salute off the eastern cape of the Bering Strait, arriving in Yokohama on 2 September. During the Second World War, the northern sea route played a vital role when the sea ports of Murmansk and Archangel opened up to take delivery of arms from America.

The following year, an expedition ship called the *Jeannette* sailed north through the Bering Strait and into the Arctic drift ice. The outcome of this expedition and the strange events that followed a few years later caused explorers to re-think their approach in a rather dramatic way.

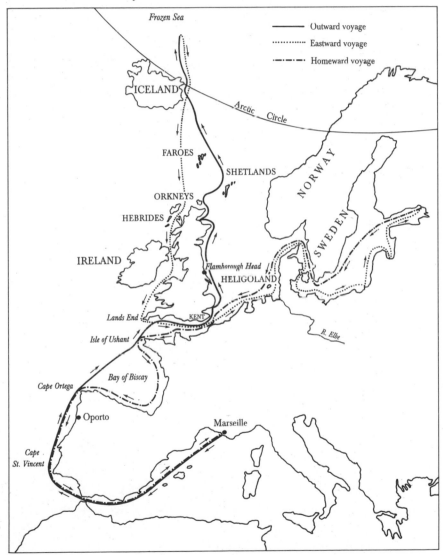

The supposed route taken by Pytheas, in the fourth century B.C.

THE RIGHT KIND
OF STUFF, TO DARE
ALL THAT MAN CAN DO

'Staunch and strong, a goodly vessel,
That can laugh at all disaster,
And with the wave and the whirlwind wrestle.'
                    –Henry Wadsworth Longfellow

George Washington De Long, a commander in the US Navy, and George Wallace Melville sailed from San Francisco north through the Bering Strait with the intention of setting up winter quarters on Wrangel Island. Their ship had been purchased by James Gordon Bennett, who was the then proprietor of the *New York Herald*, from Sir Allen Young in London. The ship was originally called the *Pandora*, but Bennett renamed her the *Jeannette*. It was a small three-masted bark with a small engine and, although much work was done to improve and strengthen her, she remained totally unsuited for the battering that she would receive from the drifting polar pack ice. Apart from it being pointed out to Bennett that changing the name of an Arctic ship was bad luck, it was an expedition doomed from the start. De Long wrote:

'Finally, however, all work came to an end, and the ship was turned over to me. I am perfectly satisfied with her. She is everything I want for the expedition, but a little small for all I want to carry in her. We must remember, however,

we are making her do the work of an expedition that has
heretofore generally required two ships. We have every
appliance for all kinds of scientific experiments; our outfit
is simply perfect, whether for ice navigation, astronomical
work, magnetic work, gravity experiments, or collections of
natural history. We have a good crew, good food, and a good
ship; and I think we have the right kind of stuff to dare all
that man can do.'

De Long had planned to sail all the way to the North Pole, as people still thought that this was possible. A great polar catastrophe
was about to unfold. The *Jeannette* steamed out of San Francisco
harbour on 8 July 1879; her first port af call was St Micheal's, on 12
August. Here, De Long took on board sledge dogs, sledges, furs
and two local Alaskan men to manage the dogs. After wasting a
great deal of time in a fruitless search for Nordenskjold, returning
in the *Vega* after completing the north-east passage, the *Jeannette*
entered the pack ice. De Long's journal for September 1879 read:

'On our course from eight last evening till seven this morning
NW (at which time we were about one hundred miles from
Wrangel Land). But at the last-named hour made the pack ice
ahead, and extending as far to the westward as we could see.
During the forenoon ran through a lot of loose ice, making a
true north course as well as possible. At 11.30, being through
the loose ice, were confronted by solid pack, which headed
us to the NE during the afternoon watch, while we were
skirting it.'

On 4 September he writes:

'The day opens calm, with a thick fog. Still at anchor to the
floe. We observed a gradual closing of the floes around, and
a seeming drift of small pieces to the south-east through the
small water spaces. The rigging is one mass of snow and frost,
presenting a beautiful sight; but, as we are more interested in
progress than beautiful sights, it has but little charm for us
. . . This is a glorious country to learn patience in. I am hoping
and praying to be able to get the ship into Herald Island, to

make winter quarters. As far as the eye can range is ice, and not only does it look as if it has never broken up and become water, but it looks as if it never would . . . This inaction is most disagreeable, and it is even more disagreeable to see no chance for a change. The only hope of the pack breaking up is the occurrence of a gale of wind. Meanwhile we are getting no nearer to Herald Island. It is unpleasant to realise that our explorations for a whole year should come to a stop on 6 September, and that at a point which a sailing ship, the *Vincennes* reached in 1855 without any difficulty. And here we are in a steamer, and beset in pack ice before we are two months out of San Francisco.'

De Long and his ship remained prisoners of the pack ice for the next few months, with ice piling up around her threatening to crush her timbers at any moment. Many narrow escapes followed, until on Monday, 24 November, the ship finally broke free. De Long writes:

'It has come at last; we are broken adrift from our floe! Suspecting what the continued action of this SW wind would be, I made sure to have the dogs securely housed on board ship before I lay down in my clothes to get some sleep. At 5 p.m., turning out, I reached the deck-house in time to see a very severe nip. The ice under the bow was piled up as high as our figurehead, and the pressure in this direction was increasing. A floe piece with a wedge shape had pierced "our" floe, and was exerting its force bravely. The ship creaked and groaned. Something had to give, for the pressure from ahead and abeam was very great. Suddenly the ship lifted from the stern, the wedge advanced, and our floe was split; and the port pressure decreasing, we were afloat on an even keel once more. The port floe moved slowly to the NE, and we followed it, our snug cradle of two and a half months being split and shattered – no longer our refuge and our strength.'

George Melville, in his book *In the Lena Delta*, describes the ice pressure:

'It was observed that, during the continuance of the wind, the whole body of ice moved evenly before it; but when it subsided, the mass that had been put in motion crowded and tumbled upon the far-off floes at rest, piling tumultuously upwards in a manner terrific to behold. It was in one of these oppressive intervals succeeding a gale, when the roar and crash of the distant masses could be distinctly heard, that the floe in which the *Jeannette* was embedded began splitting in all directions. The placid and almost level surface of ice suddenly heaved and swelled into great hills, buzzing and wheezing dolefully. Giant blocks pitched and rolled as though controlled by invisible hands; and the vast compressing bodies shrieked a shrill and horrible song that curdled the blood. On came the frozen waves, nearer and nearer. Seams ran and rattled across them with a thundering boom, while, silent and awe struck, we watched their terrible progress. Sunk in an amphitheatre about five-eighths of a mile in diameter lay the ship, the bank of moving ice puffed in places to a height of fifty feet, gradually enclosing her on all sides . . . Preparations were made for her abandonment; but – what then? If the mighty circle continued to decrease, escape was hopeless, death inevitable. To think of scrambling up the slippery sides of the rolling mass would be equal folly with an attempt to scale the falling waters of Niagara.'

It was not long before the *Jeannette* became fast in the ice once more. The short Arctic summer was over and ice 'gripped the ship nearly down to her keel.' She drifted helplessly through the long dark polar winter, until on 26 January 1880 the sun returned again. The following summer passed and still the ice held on to the *Jeannette*; De Long wrote;

'People beset in the pack ice before always drifted somewhere to some land; but we are drifting about like a modern *Flying Dutchman*, never getting anywhere, but always on the move. Coals are burning up, food is being consumed, the pumps are still going, and thirty-three people are wearing out their lives and souls like men doomed to imprisonment for life.'

Eventually, after twenty months drifting in the polar pack, De Long heard the cry 'Land!' Two small islands came into view, which De Long named Jeannette and Henrietta. On 12 June 1881, the position of the *Jeannette* was 77°71'N, 155°48'E, close to Bennett Island. The build-up of pressure around the ship was now intense and it became clear to De Long that his ship was doomed. De Long writes:

> 'At five o'clock the pressure was renewed, and continued with tremendous force, the ship cracking in every part. The spar-deck began to buckle up, and the starboard side seemed again on the point of coming in. Orders were now given to get out provisions, clothing, bedding, ship's books and papers, and to remove all sick to a place of safety. While engaged in this work, another tremendous pressure was received, and at 6 p.m. it was found that the ship was beginning to fill. From that time forward every effort was devoted to getting provisions, etc., on the ice, and it was not desisted from until the water had risen to the spar-deck, the ship being heeled to starboard about 30°. The entire starboard side of the spar-deck was submerged, the rail being under water, and the waterline reaching to the hatch-coamings. The starboard side was evidently broken-in abreast the mainmast, and the ship was settling fast. Our ensign had been hoisted at the mizzen, and every preparation made for abandoning; at 8 p.m. everybody was ordered to leave the ship. Assembling on the floe, we dragged all our boats and provisions clear of bad cracks, and prepared to camp down for the night'.

On 13 June 1881, the *Jeannette* finally went down, leaving only the foremast showing above the water. Melville writes:

> 'During the early hours of the morning' Kuehne, the watch, had attentively observed the ship as she swayed to and fro, creaking and groaning with the movements of the ice. Towards four o'clock, the hour for him to summon his relief, he suddenly announced, in addition to his stage whisper to Bartlett, 'Turn out if you want to see the last of the *Jeannette*.

There she goes! There she goes!' Most of us barely had time to arise and look out, when amid the rattling and banging of her timbers and ironwork, the ship righted and stood almost upright; the floes that had come in and crushed her slowly backed off; and as she sank with slightly accelerated velocity, the yardarms were stripped and broken upwards parallel to the masts; and so, like a giant gaunt skeleton, its hands clasped above its head, she plunged out of sight. Those of us who saw her go down did so with mingled feelings of sadness and relief. We were so utterly isolated, beyond any rational hope of aid; with our proper means of escape, to which so many pleasant associations attached, destroyed before our eyes; and hence it was no wonder we felt lonely, and in a sense that few can appreciate. But we were satisfied, since we knew full well that the ship's usefulness had long ago passed away, and we could now start at once, the sooner the better, on our long march south.'

From here on De Long and his crew hauled their ship's boats over the ice, in an attempt to reach the New Siberian Islands and then on to the Lena Delta and with a bit of good fortune, safety. They travelled by night – that is between 6 p.m. and 6 a.m., as there was no darkness at this time of year – following a strict travel routine:

Call all hands	4.30 p.m.
Breakfast	5 p.m.
Break camp	5.40 p.m.
Under-way	6 p.m.
Halt	11.30 p.m.
Dinner	Midnight
Pack up	12.40 a.m.
Under-way	1 a.m.
Halt, pitch camp	6 a.m.
Lime juice	6 a.m.
Supper	6.30 a.m.
Set watch, pipe down, turn in	7 a.m.

The journey over the ice was long and tedious, high pressure ridges and open water causing the sledges and boats to be ferried many times; De Long writes:

> 'Now that we have two of the loads lightened, and the dogs' work increased, I find that the men have to go over the same ground four times each minus one, and the dogs five times minus one. This means, that at the first trip they bring up two sleds; second trip, two sleds; third trip, first cutter; fourth trip, second cutter and whale boat; and, generally speaking, they and the dog sleds finish the day's work at the same time. One mile made, therefore, means seven miles travelled by men and nine by sleds, what with coming and going, and a constant succession of ferriages and bridges fell to our lot. The wind seemed very searching, and finally our accustomed fog and misty rain set in, making us wet as well as cold.'

They had no alternative: either haul the boats and sleds to safety, or die. By now the journey must have seemed never-ending, with no let-up from the hard labour in sight. The heavy weights which the men had to drag through such a jumbled maze of fractured ice must have made every part of their being ache. Melville describes the state of the men's footwear:

> 'Many and many times, after a day's march, have I seen no less than six men standing with their bare feet on the ice, having worn off the soles of their stockings. Nor would it have been possible to avoid this, since we could not carry enough 'oog-joog' skin, of which moccasin soles are made, to have kept alone our boots in repair. Many were the devices to which we resorted in order to keep our feet off the ice. At first we made soles by sewing patch upon patch of 'oog-joog'. Then we tried the leather of the oar-looms, but it was too slippery, as was also the sheet rubber, which some of the men had thrown away. We used canvas; sewed our knapsack straps into little patches for our heels and the balls of our feet; plaited rope-yarns, hemp and manilla into a similar protection, with soles of wood; and plaited whole mats the shape of our feet.

A large number marched with their toes protruding through their moccasins; some with the 'uppers' full of holes, out of which the water and slush spurted at every step. Yet no one murmured so long as his feet were clear of the ice, and I have here to say that no ship's company ever endured such severe toil with such little complaint. Another crew perhaps may be found to do as well, but never better!'

Ninety days after the *Jeannette* went down, De Long and his crew reached Semonovski Island in the New Siberian Islands. Here the captain left a record, which told of the events leading to his visit and how, with only seven days' provisions left, they were hoping to reach some settlement on the Lena River. While on the island some of the crew managed to shoot a deer, which must have given the party a great morale boost. On the morning of 12 September thirty-three people comprising officers and crew left Semonovski Island in three ship's boats. The boats met with a terrible storm. At one point the boats were almost sunk by waves breaking over the gunwales and almost crushed by an ice floe. At the start of the journey they travelled linked together in convoy, but the boats were tossed about by the wild waves and the unequal strain of the tow ropes. Drenched and soaked to the skin they struggled on.

Eventually the boats separated, one cutter commanded by the captain, the other cutter by Cripps, and the whale boat by Melville. Cripps's boat was never seen again.

De Long had given the order that should the boats be separated, then each should make the best way they could to a settlement on the Lena Delta. On 16 September De Long in his small boat made landfall at the Lena Delta. Here De Long and his men abandoned the boat and waded one and a half miles ashore carrying their provisions with them. The nearest settlement to them was thought to be around ninety-five miles away and it was decided that two of the party would go forward to the settlement and bring help. On 9 October, Nindemann and Noros started out, with those who remained only strong enough to raise a feeble cheer. One by one the remaining men died. On the 123rd day of his journey De Long writes:

'Missed Lee. Went down a hole in the bank and camped. Sent back for Lee. He had turned back, lain down and was ready to die. All united in saying the Lord's Prayer and Creed after supper. Living gale of wind. Horrible night.'

His diary entries carry on; despairing and hopeless he writes:

'Oct. 17, Monday – one hundred and twenty-seventh day. Alexey dying. Doctor baptised him. Read prayers for the sick. Mr Collins' birthday – forty years old. About sunset Alexey died. Exhaustion from starvation.
Oct. 22, Saturday – one hundred and thirty-second day. Too weak to carry bodies of Lee and Kaack out on the ice. The doctor, Collins, and I carried them around the corner, out of sight. Then my eye closed up.'

De Long's last entry read:

'Oct. 30, Sunday – one hundred and fortieth day. Boyd and Gortz died during the night. Mr Collins dying.'

In the meantime, Nindermann and Noros were still alive and, carrying out the order given to them by their captain, they finally reached the settlement of Ku Mark Surt. Ironically, it is said that here they could not make themselves understood to the natives, so had to travel further to the settlement at Belun, where they were fortunate to meet up with Melville and his party. After hearing of the plight of De Long and what was left of his party, Melville quickly organised a group of Cossacks and set out to rescue De Long.

It seems almost unbelievable that Melville, after such a long, desperate struggle since leaving the *Jeannette*, would still have the drive, determination and courage to set off once more into the Arctic wilderness. Melville writes:

'Ah! It was cold! The blast seemed to go clean through me . . . We laboured along among the boulders of ice for more than a mile, and then opening out at length into the clear bed of the river, we turned to the west bank where there was a sufficient snowfall; and, digging a hole, as before, in the drift, we set up our sleds to the windward and crawled, cold, supperless into our sleeping bags, beyond the fiercest fury of the storm . . . It is very Arctic weather when the sleeper's nose is frozen, and his thumb, when he tries to thaw out his nose by holding it in the palm of his hand, with thumb extended and exposed; which thumb he later on thrusts into his mouth to thaw, and so on, *ad nauseam*. Thus we lay through the night, and when day came it brought a lull to the storm; and since we could not hope to push forward, we remained all awful day without food, camped and motionless, with the poor dogs cuddled shivering on top to keep us warm.'

Melville and his rescue party finally came upon the dead bodies of De Long and his men. When all had been found they were buried on a promontory near to where they had been found, which is now known as 'Monument Point'. When Gordon Bennett received information about the fate of De Long and the *Jeannette* in October, he ran the following headline in the *New York Herald* – POLAR CATASTROPHE: THE DE LONG EXPEDITION CRUSHED BY THE ICE.

Around three and a half years after the *Jeannette* was crushed in the Siberian ocean, something strange happened. Relics from the ship started to be washed up on the south-east coast of Greenland. These relics, therefore, must have drifted all the way across the Arctic ocean, possibly across the North Pole itself. The discovery of the *Jeannette* relics gave rise to the theory that a trans-polar drift stream must exist and that if a ship, strong enough to withstand the pressure of the drifting ice, could be put into the ice off the Siberian coast, then it should eventually drift across the Pole and then on into the north Atlantic ocean. It was a fascinating theory, and it was to be another ten years before an expedition put this theory to the test.

In 1879, Dr Georg von Neumayer presided over the International Polar Conference in Hamburg. Representatives from eleven other nations were present when it was decided to mount the first International Polar Year for 1882–83. Fifty polar stations were set up with the United States being assigned the areas accessible via Smith Sound. So, in 1881 Lieutenant Adolphus Washington Greely of the US Army was put in charge of the American expedition. Greely and his men were taken to Lady Franklin Bay in the *Proteus* under the command of Captain Richard Pike. At Discovery Harbour, Greely, along with twenty-four men, built a base which he named Fort Conger. During their two-year stay Greely sent sledge parties out to explore Grant Land and Grinnel Land, as it was known then (now Ellesmere Island), and one across to Greenland. The Greenland journey was led by Lieutenant James Booth Lockwood accompanied by David Brainard and an Inuit called Christiansen. Travelling with only one dog sledge and twenty-five days' food they reached latitude 83°24'N, at what is now Lockwood Island north of Greenland.

Unfortunately, relief ships failed to reach Greely at the end of his expedition, which forced him into making the decision to attempt a return journey south in his steam-driven launch and two barks. There followed a fearful journey south to Cape Sabine, where Greely and his men built a stone hut and awaited any signs of a relief ship. Scurvy broke out and rations ran low. One by one the men started to die. One man committed suicide, while another was executed for stealing another man's food. They were even thought to have fallen into cannibalism. The crew of a sealing ship, the *Thetis*, eventually discovered six survivors on 22 June 1884. The sight which presented itself to them was described by Dr R. Wheeler in his book *The Polar Hunters*:

> 'The tent had fallen down, none of those underneath could move. One of the rescuers then took his knife, made a rip in the cloth and looked inside; a man with his jaw hanging free and glassy eyes seemed dead. Ellison, who was nothing more than a human wreck, without hands or feet, had a spoon attached to the stump of his right arm. Greely was on his hands and knees, with long hair in pigtails; he resembled a skeleton, and all his joints were bulbous and swollen. He could not stand up. The three others were scarcely better off. All the food that remained in the tent were two repulsive-looking cans of jelly, which had been obtained by boiling strips cut from their sealskin clothing.'

Surprisingly, despite all he had gone through, Greely survived and lived to become a General.

The North Pole remained the 'centre of dreams' and a much longed for goal which sat deep in the hearts of every polar explorer, even though every serious attempt thus far had failed far short of its ultimate objective and, in many cases, met with premature disaster. However, progress was being made. The honour of being able to say that you have been further north than any other man was still being contested, with a slow succession of expeditions taking their turn at nibbling away the degrees of latitude.

Even in the late nineteenth century, scientists were still pretty unsure as to the exact nature of the Pole itself. No one had ever been there, which meant that all deductions at that time were nothing more than the result of much educated guesswork. Of course, speculation was rife. Scientists deduced that the lowness of temperature in the locality of the Pole must be of such an intensity, that in winter it would, without doubt, freeze the blood in a man's veins. Even in the summer season, it was thought that it would be impossible for human life to be sustained there. Theories of the existence of land at the highest latitudes were still very common and it was even thought that in the region of the Pole itself, explorers would encounter large areas of ice-covered land similar to that found in Antarctica.

Following the ill-fated Greely and *Jeannette* expeditions, high-latitude exploration appeared to fall from favour among the eminent Arctic adventurers of the time; that is until 1892, when a young Norwegian called Fridtjof Nansen revealed his plans to the world. Nansen was without doubt the archetypal polar explorer. Standing over six feet tall, he had fair hair and clear blue eyes which were said to be as keen as steel. His muscular, well made frame was strong and supple, whilst, as is absolutely vital for a polar explorer, his physical health was perfect. A true 'Viking' and expert skier, Nansen had already proved his worth back in 1888, when he led a small expedition which was to make the first ever complete crossing of the Greenland ice cap from Umivik on the east coast, across to Godthaab on the west coast.

For some time now, Nansen had known about the strange tale

of the *Jeannette* and the fact that in 1884, wreckage debris and relics from the ship were washed up on the south-west tip of Greenland. Among these relics were items of clothing belonging to Noros and Nindemann, the only men to survive out of De Long's boat party. A number of biscuit boxes and a list of stores in De Long's own handwriting were also found. Since the *Jeannette* had been lost just north of the New Siberian Islands in 1881, it was clear that the wreckage had taken three full years to drift first north, then south across the Arctic ocean and eventually out into the north Atlantic before being washed up on the Greenland shoreline. It seemed fair for Nansen to assume that all these bits of flotsam from the *Jeannette* may even have drifted across the Pole itself.

Inspired by the story of the *Jeannette* relics, Nansen formulated a plan to utilise this 'trans-polar drift' to an expedition's advantage, working on the principle that what happened to the *Jeannette* wreckage, could also happen to a whole ship. At 12.30 p.m. on 24 June 1883, Nansen set sail from Norway in a specially designed ship called the *Fram*. His plan was to sail to a point as close to the place where the *Jeannette* sank as possible and then to let the Arctic drift ice take the ship in its grip. Once ice-bound, the ship would then drift with the pack ice in the same way as the *Jeannette* wreckage did in June 1881. Unfortunately, the *Fram* became ice-bound some three hundred miles west of the *Jeannette's* last position, and after two years of drifting the ship reached 84°04'N, 356 nautical miles south of the Pole. No other ship had been this far north.

On 14 March 1895, Nansen, in company with Lieutenant Hjalmar Johansen, left the *Fram* and it was to be a long time before they saw her again. For twenty-five days they drove their dog teams north towards the Pole. Several times Johansen fell through the ice and got soaked, and had to carry on in frozen clothes. Nansen's equipment was not functioning as well as he had expected and the two men were now at the mercy of any slight hitch. On 7 April, Nansen said that he would travel no further. He took a sun observation and calculated that they had reached 86°13'N. They were the most northerly inhabitants of the world.

On 8 April 1895, the two men turned around and headed south.

It was to be a gruelling journey. Eventually they reached Cape Flora in Franz Josef Land where they were fortunate to come across an English expedition led by Frederick Jackson. Jackson greeted Nansen with a hearty 'How do you do? I'm immensely glad to see you.' Nansen replied, 'Thank you. I also.'

'Have you a ship here?'

'No. My ship is not here.'

'How many are there of you?'

'I have a companion at the ice edge.'

All the time Jackson stared at Nansen's face and thought that he recognised him.

'Aren't you Nansen?'

'Yes I am.'

'By jove, I am awfully glad to see you!'

Then they shook hands once more.

On his return to Norway, Nansen was told that while he had been away the X-ray had been discovered and that a Swede called Andrée was intending to reach the North Pole by balloon.

Salomon August Andrée had the very romantic idea of flying to the North Pole by gas-filled balloon. Andrée had also based his plan on the theory of 'drift', but unlike Nansen's theory which was purely concerned with ice drift, Andrée's plan was to take advantage of drifting air currents. In 1886, the year the *Fram* finally broke free from the polar drift ice, Andrée, along with his two friends, Knut Hjalmar Ferdinand Fraenkel and Dr Nils Strindberg, was in the Arctic waiting patiently for the right conditions to start his flight north. Unfortunately, he failed to get away that year. The following year, Andrée returned to the Arctic and from his base on Dane's Island in Spitzbergen, he prepared for another attempt. On 11 July 1897, the air conditions seemed to be just right for their proposed flight across the Arctic Ocean. The hydrogen-filled balloon rose out of the balloon house, which they had built at Dane's Island, and into an air current which was moving towards the north. The support team gave a cheer as the balloon floated steadily northwards and out of sight. It was expected that during the next week or so, Andrée's balloon would pass over the Pole and continue across the polar sea to descend somewhere in northern Siberia. The whole world awaited news, but weeks turned into months and then into years, without any contact from Andrée.

Thirty-three years later, a small wooden sloop called the SS *Bratvaag*, under the command of Peder Eliassen, sailed close to White Island, to the north-east of Spitzbergen. Normally the *Bratvaag* would have been hunting seals at this time of year, but this year she had been hired by the Norwegian Svalbard and Polar Research Institution and was carrying a group of scientists onboard. At White Island, the scientists went ashore in search of geological and botanical samples. Little did they know, that they would also discover the fate of Andrée and his comrades.

On the island, they found the last camp of the Andrée expedition along with the remains of all three men. When news of the discovery got back to Sweden, a group of journalists travelled to White Island and during this visit one of them found the expedition diaries. These revealed the tragic story of how they had come down on the ice on 14 July 1897 at 82°55'N, 30°E. From this position the three men had travelled on foot over the drifting ice, making landfall on White Island on 5 October the same year. They had set up a winter camp on the island, but inexplicably, on 17 October, the expedition notes stop. The cause of their deaths is still a mystery.

In 1898, an American called Robert Edwin Peary sailed north through Smith Sound on the east coast of Ellesmere Island, Canada, in a ship called the *Windward*. Leaving the ship at Cape D'Urville, Peary, along with Dr Dedrick, Matt Henson and several Eskimo hunters, sledged north to General Greely's old base at Fort Conger. His intention was to occupy the base as a forward staging post, ready for an attempt at the Pole. The *Fram*, under the command of Otto Sverdrup, had also arrived in the area and, believing that Sverdrup also intended to use Fort Conger, Peary decided to try and beat him to it. Starting out earlier than he had planned, Peary and his party had a hard journey to Fort Conger travelling along the coastal ice, as it was still winter and too dark for safe travel on the sea ice. The cold was intense; they ran out of food and were obliged to kill a dog to survive. When they eventually reached Fort Conger, they were on the point of starvation and Peary was suffering from severe frostbite in both feet. Peary wrote:

> 'A little remaining oil enabled me, by the light of our sledge cooker, to find the range [fireplace] and the stove in the officers' quarters, and after some difficulty fires were started in both. When this was accomplished, a suspicious "wooden" feeling in my right foot led me to have my kamiks [seal-skin boots] pulled off, and I found to my annoyance that both feet were frosted.'

Matt Henson's account of Peary's frostbite injury goes into greater detail, describing how after removing Peary's boots he saw that his legs were 'bloodless white' up to the knee, and when the undershoes were removed several of his toes from each foot clung to the hide and snapped off at the first joint. When he was asked why he didn't tell anyone that his feet were frozen, he replied: 'There's no time to pamper sick men on the trail. Besides, a few toes aren't much to give to achieve the Pole.'

Dr Dedrick removed parts of seven of Peary's toes, before lashing him on to a sledge and travelling the two hundred and fifty miles back to the ship. Once onboard ship, Peary underwent further amputations, which left him with only the little toe on each foot. In spite of his horrific injuries he made several more journeys, even before the stumps of his toes had had time to heal, the most notable of them being from Fort Conger north-east along the northern coast of Greenland to Cape Wyckoff. This journey covered over eight hundred miles and determined Cape Morris Jesup as the most northerly point of Greenland, at 83°39'N. Peary went as far as 83°50'N, and on his way back to base he picked up the document left by Lockwood seventeen years earlier.

On the other side of the Arctic, an Italian expedition led by Prince Luigi Amandeo, the Duke of Abruzzi, had, on the advice of Nansen, purchased a whaling ship called the *Jason*. The ship was refitted and renamed the *Stella Polare* ('Pole Star'). There is an old seafaring superstition about renaming a ship: no matter how good she may have been in the past, no matter how trustworthy, to sail her under a new name would be to ensure disaster. She set sail from Norway under the command of Captain Umberto Cagni and headed for Teplitz Bay in Franz Josef Land. On her deck she carried a hundred and twenty sledge dogs. Frederick Jackson's book, *A Thousand Days in the Arctic*, had just been published, so Cagni had the advantage of Jackson's new chart of Franz Josef Land.

The duke's plan was quite simplistic, but dangerously impractical. He intended to make a direct assault on the Pole in a succession of stages. At the end of each stage, a depot of food and fuel would be left to support the party on its return journey, and at these stages some of the men would return to the ship. The plan aimed to put four men in a position from which they could make a final dash for the Pole and return to the ship picking up the pre-placed depots along the way. This was, of course, an unworkable plan, as the drift of the ice would move the depots making them impossible to find on their return from the Pole. Undaunted, the duke and his men prepared for the march on the Pole. Unfortunately, during the winter the duke became severely frostbitten in his fingers and the expedition doctor was obliged to remove the tips of two of them. This made the duke unfit to take part in the main journey.

After one false start in February, when they were beaten back by the cold, they made a good start on 11 March 1901. The state of the ice was terrible, with great broken ridges barring their route. On 21 March, three men were sent back to the ship, but were never seen again. Meanwhile, the polar party pressed on, unaware that the three men were lost. Finally, the party was reduced to only four men, who pushed on past the furthest north record set by Nansen. Living off dog flesh, the party pushed on even further, and on 24 April reached 86°33′N. They had set a new record and all elected to return to the ship.

Their return journey was a nightmare of broken, drifting ice. Most of the time they were at the mercy of the wind, drifting on small islands of ice. Over one hundred days after leaving the ship, the four men spent and on the verge of starvation, they arrived at Teplitz Bay. They had travelled a total of over 750 miles.

The year 1902 saw Peary make his first definite bid to reach the

Pole. On 24 March Peary, Henson and a support team of Eskimo hunters left Fort Conger with nine sledges and dog teams. They followed the coast to the north as far as Cape Hecla, arriving on 6 April. From here the party struck out across the polar pack ice to the north. The ice was covered with deep soft snow, making it hard going for both men and dogs, who were driven almost to exhaustion each day. On 20 April, Peary reached 84°17′N. Peary wrote in his diary: 'The game is off, my dream of sixteen years is ended. I have made the best fight I knew; I believe it has been a good one, but I cannot accomplish the impossible.' Peary turned his dog teams around and travelled homeward, bringing to an end his first bid for the laurels of the grim north.

Back home in America, Morris K. Jesup had persuaded a small group of millionaires to form a rather élite club which he called the 'Peary Arctic Club'. The sole objective of the club was to arrange finances for 'an extended scheme of exploration', which would result in the 'attainment of the North Pole'. However, following Peary's failures over the last four years, the club members were becoming discouraged and wanted to see results from their investments. Peary wrote to all the club members, asking them to consider continuing their support for one more 'final' expedition.

Peary's plan was to construct a ship strong enough to force a passage to a point near to Floeberg Beach, on the northern side of Ellesmere Island, near to the site of the *Alert's* winter quarters. Working on the 'Peary system', that he could make six degrees' progress to the north when he started out from 78°N, it would seem perfectly reasonable to say that should he be able to start out from 84°N, then he should in theory be able to reach the Pole. In the end, it was Morris Jesup himself who made the offer to guarantee the building of a suitable ship for Peary's expedition, and he donated $25,000 which was half the cost of the ship. The donation was given on the understanding that Peary would endeavour to raise the outstanding balance of $25,000. Peary knew that he stood little chance of raising this amount. Fortunately for Peary, Mr Charles Dix, of the McKay & Dix shipyard, offered 'on his own responsibility' to purchase all the necessary timber, only hoping that Peary could raise the money to pay him back.

In March 1905 the ship was launched and named the *Roosevelt* She was perfect for the task ahead and her construction had been supervised by Peary himself at every stage. The *Roosevelt* sailed out of New York Harbour on 16 July 1905 and headed north for Ellesmere Island, under the command of Captain Robert (Bob) A. Bartlett. The ship forced her way north through the heavy pack ice of Smith Sound and on to Cape Sheridan on the northern coast of Ellesmere Island. The north coast of Ellesmere Island is one of the remotest places on Earth. In 1985, I was dropped off by aircraft on Ward Hunt Island, which is about a hundred miles to the west of Cape Sheridan, and its raw wildness has to be seen to be believed. The surroundings make you feel less than insignificant, and all man's technological power seems to dwindle to almost nothing in comparison with the power of nature in the remote region. So at last Peary had reached the position he had dreamed of. His ship was frozen in at about 82°30'N. and was fully equipped for a final dash to the Pole in the following spring.

Peary set his plan into action on 19 February 1906; twenty-eight men with 120 dogs left the *Roosevelt* for the Pole. Peary was now fifty years old and had decided to try and set up a base north of Cagni's furthest north record, and then carry on to the Pole itself. He planned to use a shuttle system of sledge teams, hauling supplies of food and fuel further and further north, until he was in a position to 'dash' for the Pole. The initial stages of the journey went exceptionally well, but after that the cold became intense and the ice and weather conditions turned bad. He pushed on regardless, until on 20 April he fixed his position to be 86°30'N, just short of Cagni's record. After another day's march, Peary claims to have reached a new furthest north of 87°06'N, a full thirty-six nautical miles' travel in one day's march. Taking into account Peary's progress so far and the ice conditions which he was encountering, together with the mysterious disappearance of the final page of his diary on which he made his calculations, it would surround his claim with serious doubt.

Peary's claim is certainly in question, but it must also be said that so is Cagni's. In these times, it was a case of having to accept the honesty and integrity of the men themselves, if we are to believe their claims. Peary wrote:

> 'I felt the mere beating of the record as but an empty bauble compared with the splendid jewel on which I had set my heart for years, and for which, on this expedition, I had almost literally been straining my life out for.'

With persistent determination, Peary planned to return for yet another battle with the grim north, and after a year's delay, once more he sailed north from New York onboard the *Roosevelt* along what was now known as the 'American route', again under the trusty command of 'Captain Bob'. The ship battled its way through now very familiar seas and again berthed at Cape Sheridan. This, for Peary, was the gateway to the Pole.

Throughout the winter, Peary and his men prepared themselves for the mammoth task ahead. In early February 1909, Captain Bob with men, sledges and dogs, left the ship and headed west along the coast to Cape Columbia. It was still dark and they were obliged to travel by lantern light along the ice foot. More teams of men and dogs from the *Roosevelt* followed, and by the time Peary himself left the ship there were seventeen crew, nineteen Eskimos, twenty-eight sledges and one hundred and forty dogs ahead of him. The whole expedition met up at Cape Columbia, and on the last day of the month Captain Bob sledged out on to the polar drift ice, to start the attack.

Temperatures during these first few critical days remained at around −50°F, which caused dark frost smoke to rise from any open water areas. Up ahead, Peary could see a large bank of black fog, indicating to him the presence of open water. It seems strange that Peary refused to learn from the experiences of other explorers such as Nansen and did not take with him material for constructing boats or kayaks. Peary was stopped for five days by this 'big lead', before it closed enough to allow them to cross. At one point, Borup was driving his sledge from one floe to another when the two masses decided to part dropping all the dogs into the water. Borup, being of powerful build, succeeded in hauling back the sledge with its 500lb load and recovering all the dogs. Peary was said to say that the sledge was, 'worth more to us out in that icy wilderness than its weight in diamonds. A man less quick and muscular might have lost the whole lot.'

Men were sent back at pre-determined points, until at 86°38′N, Marvin and two Eskimos were sent back. At last, Peary had for certain sledged past the Italian record and apart from a few days lost, everything was going to plan. As Marvin left for his return journey, Peary bid him farewell and said: 'Be careful of the leads, my boy!' Little did he know that he would never see him again. Further north, Captain Bob was forging ahead and was rapidly approaching 87°06′N, which was Peary's furthest north claim, and in due course passed it. To the south, Peary was pressing forward and would soon catch up.

Peary now had the best chance of reaching the Pole. He was well supplied and his dogs were still in reasonably good condition, with only 180 nautical miles between him and his goal. At 87°47′N, Peary ordered Captain Bob back to the ship. He was deeply disappointed as he had led most of the way from the coast and was still in good spirits. He had often left Peary behind by setting a fast pace. Understandably, he very much wanted to remain with the last group and continue to the Pole. He was certainly fit enough, but the final party had already been selected and Peary felt unable to add another. On the day Captain Bob started back, the expedition stood only 133 nautical miles from the Pole. The final party consisted of Peary, Matt Henson and four Eskimos – Egingwah, Ootah, Seegloo and Ooqueah. They had five sledges with forty dogs which were all in good condition, and it was Peary's plan to cover the remaining distance in under a week. They had with them food and fuel for forty days, but could stretch it to sixty if necessary.

On 5 April, Peary checked his position to be 89°25′N, only thirty-five nautical miles from the Pole. Peary wrote: 'I had not dared to hope for such progress; still the biting cold would have been impossible to face by anyone not fortified by an inflexible purpose.' On 6 April, Peary force-marched for twelve hours, with only one stop for food and his position was now 89°57′N, just three nautical miles from the Pole. From this position, the North Pole would actually be in sight. Peary claims to have had sledges around to fix the Pole exactly, but if he was that close to the Pole it would have seemed pointless. Peary wrote in his diary: 'The Pole at last. The prize of three centuries. My dream and ambition for twenty-three years. Mine at last! I cannot bring myself to realize it. It seems all so simple and so commonplace.'

Peary returned to America and a hero's welcome, which was to be tarnished by an announcement from Dr Frederick Cook, that he had reached the North Pole on 21 April 1908. This was disbelieved at the time and is still being disputed. It started a controversy which still rumbles on to this day, mainly because neither man could provide sound, positive and indisputable evidence of having reached the Pole.

This golden age of Arctic exploration passed with terrific suffering and loss of life. Conditions endured by the crews of expedition ships were, at times, hideously squalid, with long hours of work on poor rations. The tragedy which struck Greely and his expedition just added to the growing list of polar disasters, along with the *Jeannette* expedition and Franklin before that. Newspapers of the time had a field day, because then, as today, bad news is always good news to the journalist. Some would write up the expedition stories as thrilling, heroic adventures, while others would slant towards the pathetic, useless loss of life as mere folly. To put pen to paper in the comfort of a newspaper office and write retrospective criticism of these men is the act of those with very little vision and understanding. Putting all journalistic misrepresentations aside, you have to salute these giants of men for their endurance, commitment and dedication to increasing man's knowledge and understanding of the planet on which we live.

Since Peary, countless expeditions have set out for the Pole, using wide and varied means of transport. Airships, airplanes of various types, dog teams, snowmobiles, on foot manhauling, on skis, by submarine, and even on a motorbike. The main thing that all these modern expeditions have in common is that they all have relied on the support of mechanical or animal transport or support from the air in one way or another to succeed. To be able to travel over the drifting ice, free of all this 'support', is now a well established method and one which gives the independent traveller the most satisfaction and pleasure. In April 1994, another Norwegian called Borge Ousland, made a superb solo journey from Cape Arctichesky in Russia to the Pole, but then used an airplane to return him to land. Just to reach the Pole is only half an expedition; Peary had to return to land under his own steam. To travel unsupported out to the Pole *and* return to land still remains one of the last great polar journeys to be made.

Otto Sverdrup, commander of the *Fram*

Fritdjof Nansen

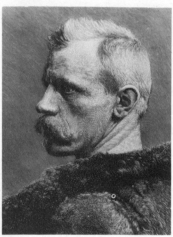

Robert Edwin Peary, who claimed to have reached the North Pole on the 6th of April 1909

A STRANGE ATTRACTION

'The true explorer does his work not for any hopes of reward or honour, but because the thing he has set himself to do is part of his being, and must be accomplished for the sake of accomplishment. And he counts lightly hardships, risks, obstacles, if only they do not bar him from his goal.'

Robert E. Peary

Unfortunately, my expedition to the Arctic in 1985 was the final straw as far as my marriage was concerned. My love of expeditioning had slowly put an increasing strain on our relationship and this last jaunt seemed to totally destroy what was left and we divorced. The process of divorce was, for me, one of the most stressful and heartbreaking events of my life. It was painful to sit and watch all that I had worked for for the past five years slowly destroyed in front of my eyes by total strangers in black gowns and wigs. My now ex-wife had also decided to live in Manchester which made it extremely difficult for me to see my son Leif, who by now was three and a half years old. I can only hope that some time in the future, when he is old enough to understand, he will want to see me and we can meet under happier circumstances.

When all the dust of my divorce had settled, I had time to consider what lay ahead. I was a serving police officer with the Derbyshire Constabulary and based in Buxton. This suited me fine, as it was right in the heart of the Peak District National Park and gave me easy access to the crags and hills which I loved so much, but first of all I had to decide what I wanted to do with the rest of my life. When I left school I worked as a scientific and industrial photographer for the National Coal Board, and since then I had often seriously thought of earning a living as a freelance photographer, specialising in wilderness photography. It looked like this would be the ideal time in my life to make the change. During my next week of night duty, I was sent over to Edale to cover the Hope Valley area. At around 2 a.m., I parked the police Land Rover outside the small police office in Edale and went in to have my break. Sitting alone in the tiny office concentrated my thoughts and I pulled over the typewriter, loaded it with a sheet of paper and typed out my letter of resignation. Before signing off duty that morning, I dropped the letter onto the superintendant's desk. It felt wonderful, I was free, but free to do what? I didn't really care; I was now freelance and in complete charge of my destiny; no more compromise between a conventional career and my love of wild places. I was totally unsure of what the future would bring and at times full of doubt and fear, but above all that I felt happier than I had been for some time. I could now base my life around the things I loved.

The next couple of years were a wonderful combination of working in the hills as an outdoor pursuits instructor and taking photographs which I sold through various picture agencies. I would often work with groups of young offenders, or children from care homes, taking them out into the hills for a taste of 'adventure'. Most of these young people had grown up the hard way in the dusty city suburbs and were well conditioned to people continually telling them how bad they were. When I gave them praise and encouragement for their efforts out on the crags or underground in a wet cave, it was quite a shock to their systems. It certainly had a very positive effect on them.

My frostbitten right foot had taken a full two years to heal and was now starting to itch. At the back end of 1986, I had taken part in a charity fund-raising event which aimed to race up the three highest mountains and descend the three deepest caves in Scotland, England and Wales in under forty-eight hours. Myself and a friend called Les Heaton eventually completed the whole course in forty-four hours fifty minutes, which included over fourteen hundred miles' driving. I lost half a stone in weight and we got into the *Guinness Book of Records*, but it gave the old feet a good run out and my mind started to wander back to the icy wastes north of Ellesmere Island. Robert Peary called this strange attraction to the polar regions 'polar fever', and I was by now suffering from the condition in a bad way. I longed to be back, but where should I go?

By 1988, I felt just about ready to take on the task of organising and preparing another expedition. I had also been commissioned to produce a book covering my experiences in Antarctica during the late seventies, so for the moment I concentrated all my energies on this project. This was my first excursion into publishing and I became totally absorbed in the process of sorting through the thousands of transparencies which I took during my two expeditions to the far south. Day after day I sat at my typewriter, and with the aid of diaries from the years when I worked in Antarctica I relived the period over again and typed out the story as I went along. By the time the *Land of the Ice King* was finished, I had made up my mind to return to Antarctica, but more specifically the island of South Georgia, where I knew there were one or two beautiful unclimbed peaks just waiting to be knocked off. I put the project to a small group of my friends, all of whom agreed that it was a good idea and that they would be interested in being part of the project.

I made an immediate start and set about the task of obtaining permission to visit the island and drumming up the required sponsorship, which I thought shouldn't be that difficult. I was very wrong. Britain was in a deepening nationwide recession and, after writing countless letters to countless potential sponsors, I drew a total blank. It would appear that to attract any major sponsorship your project must be an attempt at a 'world first', to be the 'fastest', 'biggest', 'deepest', 'longest'; oh, and by the way, there must be a bikini-clad woman in the team! Obtaining permission to travel to South Georgia also turned out to be more difficult than I at first thought. Red tape, bureaucracy and every other conceivable obstacle seemed to be put in front of us, until eventually I had to hold up my hands and surrender. The Arctic became more and more attractive by the day.

Each year I followed the progress of various Arctic expeditions and longed to be there with them, but was amazed as year after year all the expeditions that invaded the far north planned to use air support, either to supply the team en route or to pick them up from the Pole on arrival. I ran through the logistics of an unsupported journey from Ward Hunt Island out to the Pole and back to land. The results were promising. The trip would require three men to haul enough food and fuel to last for between ninety and a hundred days, covering around 1,200 nautical miles on the round trip. Unsupported journeys of this length and duration have been achieved in the past, so in theory a North Pole expedition should have no need for air support at all.

Punch Wilson, Alan Gamble and myself met up one evening at the Bakers Arms in Buxton and over a couple of pints we went through the possibilities of making a journey from the coast of the Arctic ocean out to the Pole and back again. At first Punch and Alan were a little dubious as to whether it would be possible or not, but after a few more pints all were in favour of giving it a go. The conversation then moved on to when we should plan to carry out the journey. At this point both Punch and Alan applied caution and quite rightly suggested that before we commit ourselves totally to the project it would be sensible for us to make a training journey. I contacted Jim Hargreaves, who had worked on Robert Swan's 'Icewalk' project, and he suggested that a good place to train and test equipment would be Iqualuit on Baffin Island. On the bay ice at Iqualuit, it is possible to recreate almost identical conditions to those found on the Arctic ocean without going to the vast expense of actually going out on to the Arctic ocean, so it was agreed that this is where we would go. The next problem was how we were to fund the trip. We put our plan to Paul Dinsdale, a local architect, and to our amazement he very kindly offered to sponsor this initial training trip.

A hectic month followed as we gathered together most of the food, fuel and equipment which we wished to test out. Roger Danes at 'Snowsled' produced a wonderful articulated double sledge for us to test out. Canadian Airlines gave us one free ticket and a good discount on the other two, plus free excess baggage, of which by now we had about half a ton. For me it was even more hectic, as I had just got married again. I had met Tracey in a local pub over a year before and at that time she was just starting a one-year postgraduate teaching course. For the next year, we saw each other every weekend and had planned to marry once she had completed her course. Fortunately, Tracey was very understanding, had come to accept my strange attraction to wild places, and had even helped as much as she could. We were living in a small one-bedroom rented flat in Buxton, which until just before we left for the Arctic resembled a warehouse, with boxes and bags of food and equipment stacked everywhere. To my eternal amazement and to her credit, Tracey put up with all the inconvenience without ever complaining once.

The flight out to Iqaluit was pretty uneventful, apart from an encounter with an over-officious Canadian Airlines official in Montreal, who refused to believe that his company would agree to transport all our excess baggage free of charge. There followed a frantic telephone call back to their London office who put him straight, and we were then allowed to check in for the flight north.

Before leaving the UK, Jim Hargreaves had given me the telephone number of Brent Boddy, who lived in Iqaluit. Brent had been to the North Pole as a member of Will Steger's expedition in 1986 and would be able to give us plenty of advice. After a short stop at Fort Chimo, we flew on north to Iqaluit. On arrival I made a telephone call from the small airport building and spoke to Brent, who came to meet us on his skidoo pulling a large box trailer sledge. Brent was a tall, lean Canadian who had moved to the north to work in the local hospital. While at Iqaluit, he met and married a local Inuit girl called Nalla, and they now have a daughter called Crystal. Brent splits his time between his work at the hospital and his own business as an 'outfitter', taking groups of tourists on dog sled trips out onto the 'land' in the winter and kayak journeys in the summertime.

After loading most of our gear onto Brent's sledge he transported us in relays over to his house, which was situated down by the edge of the sea ice. We put up our tent in Brent's 'backyard' next to his dog spans and he invited us into his home for coffee. Brent was a mine of information and we all learned a lot from him. He introduced us to 'Muk-Tuk', which is raw, frozen whale skin. Muk-Tuk has a very high fat content, making it a good winter food which the Inuit cut up into small cubes and eat as a snack. All through that first night Brent's sled dogs howled and brought back many happy memories of my days working with dogs in Antarctica. There is something quite eerie but strangely soothing when around forty husky dogs decide to howl at the moon all at the same time. Usually one will start and slowly more will join in, until the whole canine choir are howling in weird unison.

For the next three weeks we hauled our sledges up and down the bay, loaded with various weights and hauling for longer and longer distances over rough and smooth ice. The temperature during our stay varied from −19°C down to −44°C, and combined with the ideal rough bay ice conditions it proved to be a perfect training ground. We tested out boots made from plastic, canvas, seal skin and moose hide and slept outside each night trying out different combinations of sleeping bags. At the conclusion of this training period, we were all confident that it would be possible to haul enough food, fuel and equipment to sustain a journey of around a hundred days, even hauling over pressure ice.

We arrived back in the UK full of confidence and with a renewed energy. By now the 'polar fever' had a strong grip on me and I got straight down to the task of hunting for a major commercial sponsor to fund our proposed expedition from Cape Columbia out to the Pole and back again. It would be an attempt at a 'world first', so we were sure that it would catch the imagination of many potential sponsors. It did, but this was 1990 and the economic recession was biting harder than ever. Every possible approach was tried, but the replies were disappointing. At one stage things looked good, as a major insurance company decided to consider the project seriously. After a lot of communications over about two months, the expedition plan made it to their shortlist of potential sponsorships for 1991, but was eventually turned down in favour of promoting a professional snooker tournament.

Every company I approached seemed to have stock answers which they used effectively to get rid of cheeky buggers with seemingly mad ideas who contact them looking for their support. The first line of defence in any major company is that solid brick wall called the 'personal assistant'. These creatures are masters of the 'get rid' technique. You would politely ask if Mr Smith was in and would it be convenient to speak to him. At this point the PA would fire the first and by far the most common defence salvo, 'I'm sorry but Mr Smith is in a meeting' or 'I'm sorry but Mr Smith is not in the office today', or the one I liked the most, 'Oh, you are so unlucky, Mr Smith has just left the office'. Each PA would then take your name and telephone number and promise sincerely that she/he would definitely put a note on Mr Smith's desk and make certain that he gives you a call the minute he returns to the office, but of course he never does. The following day, you call back to be told, 'Did he not call you? Oh, I am sorry, I did give him your number, but now he has gone on holiday for two weeks.'

On the equipment side, we were having far more luck. Most of the equipment suppliers we contacted were more than helpful and did their very best to help, even though they are inundated each day by requests for sponsorship from expeditions, including requests from that professional expedition machine called Sir Ranulph Fiennes. It appeared to the nation that Ranulph Fiennes and Mike Stroud spent most of the second half of the nineteen eighties attempting to walk one way to the North Pole. They were never successful, but their expeditions were tremendous efforts and to a large extent ironed out a lot of ambiguities in the 'unsupported' debate. However, this had a strange effect on other, probably much more worthy, expeditions when it came to searching for sponsorship. Time and time again we came up against the same statements: 'If Fiennes and Stroud can't get to the Pole, how the hell do you think you can?' or 'I thought Fiennes and Stroud had already done that?'

For a further eighteen months, Punch and I continued to search for that one elusive sponsor. Now and then we would be very optimistic when a company showed interest, and after meetings and presentations to the marketing managers our hopes would be dashed due to some financial restraint or other. Then all of a sudden I had a breakthrough: a Sunday newspaper called *The Sunday Correspondent* offered the expedition £18,000 for the story, which we gratefully accepted; but then two weeks later the paper went into liquidation!

By early 1992, Tracey and I were busy working on a small cottage which we had bought situated on the outskirts of Buxton. We were feeling very excited as Tracey had just found out that she was pregnant. The following September, and after a long, painful labour, Tracey gave birth to a five-pound-ten-ounce baby daughter. Fortunately, I was able to be there at the birth, holding Tracey's hand throughout the whole event. I sat by the bedside with tears in my eyes as I watched my little daughter delivered into the world, and I can remember being almost shocked by the volume of that first squeaky cry. After bandying a number of names about we both settled on Hannah.

The next few months were idyllic in many ways. Tracey was on maternity leave and I, being freelance, could spend lots of time with both of them. My photography work was slowly building up and I was picking up some work on 'action-based' management training courses, which seemed to be very popular at the time. I would spend weeks at a time belting around the Peak District with minibuses full of usually pretty unfit junior and middle managers from a variety of companies, trying to get them to work together as a team. I still found time to search for that single elusive sponsor which would give Punch and I the chance of going for the Pole; but it was looking like we would never get a sponsor for the expedition, and without it all the planning and preparations would remain nothing but dreams.

THE DREAM
BECOMES REALITY

'But, what would life be without its dreams?'
Fridtjof Nansen

O ne day the telephone rang. 'Hi Clive, it's Steve Martin.'
'Not the Steve Martin of Hollywood fame I hope?'
'No, same name but different bank account.'
I had known Steve for some time now and we met up from time
to time for a drink or two and a chat, mainly revolving around
polar expeditions. Steve had been a professional sailor, crewing
on yachts in various places around the world, before deciding to
go to Antarctica. Steve applied to the British Antarctic Survey and
was duly called for an interview with Eric Salmon at the Survey's
headquarters in Cambridge. During the interview the telephone
rang. It was the master of the Royal Research ship *John Biscoe*,
which was berthed at Liverpool for her refit prior to heading south.
There was a short conversation and Eric wrote down a telephone
number which was the ship's contact number in Liverpool. Eric
then excused himself from the interview for a moment. While
Eric was out of the office Steve copied the number from his
pad. Unfortunately Steve didn't get the job with the Survey,
but he did make good use of the telephone number. He called
the ship's office and somehow managed to get himself signed on
as a 'greaser' in the engine room for the duration of the ship's
forthcoming Antarctic tour.

The following year, Steve went south to South Georgia where he was to take over the roll of base commander for the southern winter. It was during this time that the Argentinian military government decided that South Georgia belonged to them and invaded. After Steve's polite diplomacy with the Argentinian warships had failed, he had no altenative but to hand over control of the island to the British armed forces. There followed a fierce battle and all base personnel were evacuated to the old abandoned whaling station at Grytviken, where they took refuge in the small church to await the outcome. Vastly outgunned and outnumbered, the British forces eventually had to surrender, but not before they had delivered one hell of a bloody nose to the unsuspecting Argentinian invaders. All the Survey members were taken prisoner along with the British soldiers. Steve was then taken to Argentina before returning to England. Undaunted, he returned to Antarctica to assist in the rebuilding of the 'Halley' station. On his return to the UK, he had taken up the offer of a place at Bristol University, where he studied medicine. After qualifying as a doctor, he had crossed the Greenland ice cap and was now keen to go to the North Pole.

The fund-raising for Steve's North Pole expedition was hitting the same problems as I had, so much so that one of the team had given up and withdrawn from the project, leaving just him and Dave Mitchell from Cumbria in the team. Steve asked if I would be interested in filling the space; I immediately agreed, but on the understanding that should no major sponsor be found by the end of October, then I would not continue. Following my conversation with Steve, I telephoned Dave Mitchell and arranged to meet. We met up at a motorway services somewhere just north of Preston and, over several cups of tea, Dave introduced to me the 'Trans-Polar Drift Stream Expedition'. Dave is one of those people you instantly like, easy-going with a sound sense of humour. After doing an apprenticeship as an electrician, he joined the British Antarctic Survey, staying with them for eight years before leaving to devote all his time to the expedition.

The whole expedition project was based on a very old theory relating to the wind-driven ice drift patterns on the Arctic ocean, the drift of the *Jeannette* relics, and the results of Nansen's *Fram* expedition. Working on the theory that if Nansen had entered the pack ice some three hundred miles further to the east then the *Fram* may well have drifted a lot closer to the pole, if not right over it, Dave pointed to a small dot on a photocopy of a map showing the entire Arctic ocean. 'That is where we start from, Henrietta Island; from there out to the Pole and, depending on ice conditions, we then carry on to the Canadian coast, and I would like to attempt it unsupported.' He gave me a sheet of paper and, on it was written 'Definition of "Unsupported"', and it said:

> From the moment which land is departed and until such time when land is reached again, no outside assistance should be used. This would include:
> 1. The removal of one or more of the team from the ice, for whatever reason, by a third party.
> 2. The receipt of any information that would directly assist the expedition's progress, e.g. ice observations and weather information etc.
> 3. The re-supply of food and equipment in addition to what the expedition started out with at the point of departure from land.
> 4. Should the expedition be, for any reason, removed from the ice, then the distance covered to the point of pick-up shall be accepted as being the 'unsupported' journey providing, that is, that points one to three have applied.

We debated for a while whether or not the use of satellite navigation equipment could be deemed as support, but in the end we came to the conclusion that the information received from such equipment could not in any way assist the expedition's progress. Knowing exactly where you are would not give you any advantage whatsoever.

Henrietta Island is the most northerly island in a group of islands, now known as the De Long Islands after the captain of the *Jeannette*. Only one other expedition had ever started out from there before, and that was the Russians under Dmitry Shparo in 1978. They used air support to re-supply the expedition and eventually reached the Pole after seventy-six days' travelling.

Dave had successfully used 'up-ski' parachutes for hauling sledges during his Greenland crossing and was very keen to make good use of any available wind on the Arctic ocean, but this time he planned to take 'parawings'. Parawings, designed and manufactured in Germany, were very light aerofoil-shaped parachutes designed specifically for pulling, and Dave had tested one out on his last tour of duty in Antarctica. I can remember reading what Sir Clements Markham had written in his journal after manhauling to 83°20'N on 1 May 1876: 'Sail-driven sledges are convenient when one is travelling on flat, soft snow, but we have rarely had the advantage of such snows . . .' Reinhold Messner, an Austrian mountaineer and adventurer, had used parawings with great success during his crossing of Antarctica. Later Ranulph Fiennes and Mike Stroud used 'up-ski' parachutes to pull their sledges during their attempt to cross Antarctica 'unsupported', but they failed 350 miles short of the coast. Dave had now used both forms of 'pulling' parachutes having used up-ski 'chutes during his crossing of Greenland with Steve, and he very much preferred the parawing. We were both agreed that should the expedition be fortunate enough to come across a freshly frozen lead, which travelled in a northerly direction, then on such smooth new ice the parawing would come into its own and be very useful indeed. Another plus for the parawing was that it only weighed around two kilos. But, could this form of wind assistance be defined as 'support'?

Dave went over the plan fully and we pooled ideas. The provisional budget for the project was £110,000, of which half would be the cost of equipment, food and fuel. The rest was to cover the cost of getting the expedition to its starting point on Henrietta Island. At this stage the expedition account boasted the grand total of £350. However, Dave's enthusiasm for the project was so contagious, that it seemed to make me forget all the knock-backs of recent years and I drove home down the M6 with a renewed determination to give the project 100 per cent of my time and effort.

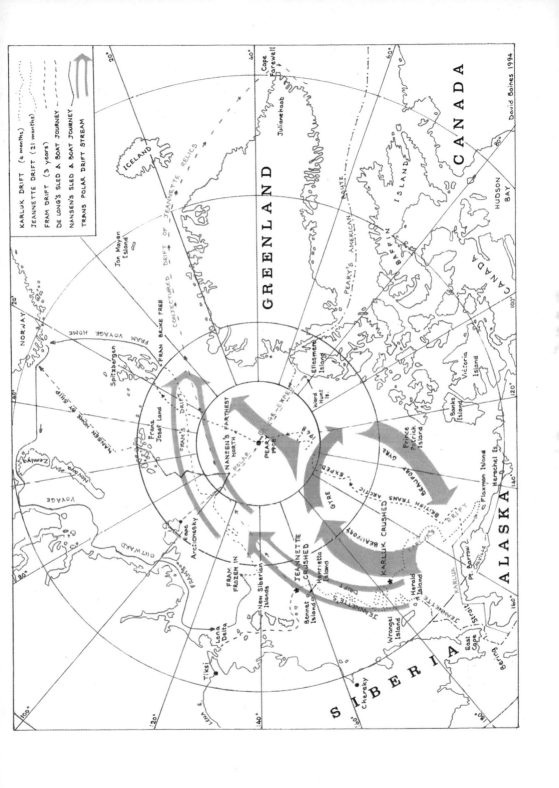

Camp 1, on the ice-shelf on the northern coast of Ward Hunt Island 1985. This was the first morning of my solo expedition.

The author and Ben Wallace-Hadrill on their return from the Magnetic North Pole region.

Dave packing 300 man-days of food in my living room, prior to sending it on to Moscow.

From left to right: Dave, Dmitry Shparo, Steve and myself, at the Adventure Club office in Moscow.

Our chartered An-12 on the ground in Moscow.

The briefing room at a military air base, somewhere in 'Bella Russia'.

Home sweet home. The radio shack which we used as our training base.

Training on the Lena river.

The author on the Lena river.

Unloading the sledges at Chokurdakh

Dr Stephen Martin

Dave Mitchell

Clive Johnson

Our two An-2 aircraft, refuelling at the New Siberian Islands.

One final flypast and we are alone.

By the end of August 1993, we had produced a new expedition proposal and had applied to the Royal Geographical Society for their approval and hopefully a grant. We also had a meeting with Tim Radford, the science editor of *The Guardian* newspaper. The meeting took place in an Indian restaurant somewhere in the middle of Stoke-on-Trent. We all sat around a table and Tim fired questions at us which he recorded on a small tape recorder placed in the middle of the table. One rather hot curry and several bottles of wine later, we said our goodbyes and Tim promised to be in touch. This he did, with the news that *The Guardian* would very much like to follow the story and liaise with the Save the Children Fund, who had adopted our expedition to help raise money for their 75th anniversary. Steve had asked Sir Vivian Fuchs if he would honour us by being one of the expedition patrons. He accepted and sent him the following letter:

> Dear Stephen Martin,
> I have been impressed by the planning of your Trans-Polar Drift Stream Expedition. The Arctic and Antarctic experience of all of you, together with quite apparent practical competence, leads me to believe in your success.
> While your medical studies of hormone release in relation to stress are of unusual importance, I also believe that your expedition will strike the imaginations of young people and demonstrate that all human endeavour is not in the interest of money making.
> I wish you every good fortune in a strenuous endeavour.
> Yours sincerely,
> V.E. Fuchs

On 10 October, Dave drove down from Gosforth to my home in Buxton and at 6 a.m. the next day we drove down to London for an interview before the Royal Geographical Society's expeditions committee. After a long search for somewhere to park, Dave and I walked through the hot dusty streets to the RGS building at Kensington Gore. After reporting to reception, we were told to wait in the hall and from there we were led upstairs and told to wait outside the committee room. Finally, the door opened and we were asked in. The room had one huge long table around which about ten people sat and opposite this table were placed two chairs. As Steve was working and unable to attend the meeting, Dave gave our apologies on his behalf and proceeded very clearly to present the expedition plan, which included a full explanation of the medical project which Steve would be carrying out during the journey. I spread out a large coloured map of the Arctic ocean on the table and explained the navigation methods and logistics. Question after question began to rain down upon us, but we had done our homework thoroughly and managed to fend them off with complete answers. Then came the unanswerable question: 'How will the expedition be funded?' At this time Steve was in serious negotiations with several companies, who were showing positive signs, but to date we still did not have a major sponsor. This had to be our answer to the committee.

After the interview Dave was very depressed, as he thought that it hadn't gone well. I, on the other hand, was optimistic and tried to put it out of my mind on the long drive home. For the next couple of weeks all three of us pushed ahead with making approaches to potential sponsors. Steve seemed to have a gift for this; even though he was working long hours at Burton Hospital, he would spend all his spare time and days off arranging meetings or writing letters. At last the letter we had been waiting for finally arrived from the RGS. They had fully approved our expedition and were also prepared to give the expedition a grant of £750. This was a major breakthrough, as the RGS approval gave the project much more credibility in the eyes of sponsors and potential sponsors.

With the approval of the RGS behind us, Steve was able to update all our potential sponsors and things started to happen. First to come onboard was Carlsberg-Tetley brewery. We all met up in Warrington at the brewery and after a long meeting with their marketing manageress, Jane Falstead, she agreed that Carlsberg would cover the cost of designing and manufacturing our sledges. This was a huge step forward, as the sledges were going to cost around £7,000. We were very happy with this, but we still needed a major sponsor and the cut-off point of the end of October was only one week away.

Steve had had a very positive meeting with the Littlewoods company in Liverpool and could now update them with the news that the expedition had RGS approval and support and also Carlsberg-Tetley had agreed to sponsor the sledges. Meanwhile Dave and I were working at getting the equipment, food and fuel together. It was a sort of limbo period, as we were not sure if the expedition was actually going ahead or not. We had to speak to equipment suppliers with total enthusiasm as if the expedition was definitely on and that we would really like to use their product. It was a 'Catch 22' situation, and one which I am sure most of the suppliers could see right through, but we had a good response, especially from British Airways.

Gary Grey at British Airways had only taken over the job of looking after sponsorships a few days before I made contact with him, but by this time I was in fast forward mode and I often wonder what he must have thought when our proposal arrived on his desk, followed by a deluge of telephone calls. In the end he very politely told me to go away and stop hassling him, so I apologised. Gary then assured me that he would give the proposal his full consideration and get back to me. Sure to his word he did, with the news that British Airways would give the expedition full sponsorship of all scheduled flights to Moscow on our outward journey and from Canada on our way home. This sponsorship would also include all our cargo which by now had mounted up to over half a ton!

I had been in contact with Dmitry Shparo in Moscow, who had been the leader of the Russian expedition which started out from Henrietta Island in 1978. Dmitry runs a company called the 'Adventure Club', which as far as I can gather exists to help disadvantaged and disabled children and adults. Another facet to his company is the organisation of logistical support for polar expeditions such as ours, and I had entered into preliminary negotiations with Dmitry who was now hard at work searching out the various possibilities available, to transport our expedition from Moscow, across middle Asia to the northern coast of Siberia, and from there to our proposed starting point of Henrietta Island. Before *perestroika*, this type of journey would have been completely out of the question, and even to think of requesting cargo space on Russian military aircraft would have been a fantasy. 'But now,' said Dmitry, 'in Russia, anything is possible.'

Things were happening and I think we all felt that the expedition was on the verge of becoming reality, and it did.

On 3 November, Steve rang me to say that he had made contact with Littlewoods and they had decided to be the expedition's major sponsor. He told me that he had had to stop in a lay-by on his way home from the meeting so that he could calm his nerves before carrying on. A few days later we all met up at my home. Steve came bursting in through the door, grinning from ear to ear, clutching a rather large bottle of champagne. We were going!

Time was now very short, and if we stood any chance at all of starting out in February both Dave and I would have to work full time on the project. But first we needed to visit Dmitry in Moscow and firm up the logistics at that end. After frantic exchanges of telephone calls and fax messages with the Russian embassy in London, they eventually rushed two visas through their extremely sluggish system. British Airways provided two return flight tickets for myself and Dave, as Steve was still hard at work at the hospital and would not be free until the end of January when his contract with the hospital ended. Dave drove down to Buxton on 26 November, and very early the next day we drove at breakneck speed down to Heathrow airport having overslept. Once in Moscow, we were met by a man called Alexander Shumilov. Alexander, or 'Sasha' as he preferred to be called, was, along with Dmitry Shparo, one of the founders of the Moscow Adventure Club. Sasha was a scientist and a prolific author and had, he proudly told me, published some thirty books. From Moscow airport we were taken in the Adventure Club 'car', which turned out to be a very rusty old Transit minibus, to the Adventure Club offices in the centre of Moscow. Before we arrived at the Adventure Club the driver of the 'car' took us into Red Square. It was a very cold evening with quite a lot of snow on the ground and, as we climbed out of the van outside St Basil's Cathedral, we were both swooped upon by a crowd of fur-clad Russian street traders, all wishing to sell us Russian-style fur hats. After taking a stroll around Red Square, we then drove on to the Adventure Club office.

On arrival at the office we were met by Dmitry and given coffee before starting our business. Dmitry started by saying that he felt very sceptical about our proposed expedition and was firmly of the opinion that to cross the Arctic ocean from Henrietta Island to Canada without air support was impossible. He also informed us of three other expeditions preparing to start out in early 1994. The first was Mitsuro Ohba from Japan; he was preparing to start out alone from Cape Arctichesky on the northern tip of Severnya Zemlya. Secondly, there was a Russian expedition that proposed to set out from Franz Josef Land, and thirdly another solo expedition by a Norwegian called Borge Ousland. This news was very interesting to me because I had previously met Borge in 1990 at Iqualuit on Baffin Island where he, along with Geir Randby and Erling Kagge, was training for a one-way journey to the North Pole starting out from Ward Hunt Island on the northern coast of Ellesmere Island. During this expedition, Geir Randby had injured his back and had to be evacuated by air from the ice. This led to a bitter argument with who else but Ranulph Fiennes and Mike Stroud who, at the same time, were also trying a one-way journey to the Pole, but from the Russian side of the Arctic ocean. Borge and Erling continued to the Pole and proudly laid claim to being the first expedition to reach the Pole totally unsupported. Fiennes and Stroud failed. Later on that year, I attended a bizarre lecture at the Royal Geographical Society in London where Erling Kagge and Mike Stroud presented their own arguments over what constituted support. Mike Stroud put forward a very weak argument which attempted to discredit the Norwegian expedition, while Kagge refused to be drawn by the sour grapes and simply said in reply:

> 'I don't plan to go into details of what is correct or incorrect about what Stroud said; obviously things are incorrect. I should remind you, you are into Captain Scott, who is a hero of everyone here including myself. On his cross at Cape Evans it says something like: "To strive, to seek, to find, and not to yield". I do think you should remember that because he is a hero of yours and if you are not happy with the way we did it, you are quite welcome to try it yourself next year.'

Both sides of the argument came over to the audience as a very weak and childish end to what were, in fact, two very commendable expeditions of which both sides should have been proud. Perhaps both sides should have asked themselves why they went to the Arctic in the first place?

After the first half of our meeting, Dmitry had arranged for us to have supper with them at the office and we were served a Siberian dish called 'pelmeney', which consisted of mealballs wrapped in a dough then boiled. As I didn't know the Russian words for 'no more, thank you', my bowl was refilled over and over again. When supper finally stopped arriving, we continued our meeting well into the night, going over possibilities, looking at maps and videos and reading expedition reports. The following day, after all our business was completed, we were treated to the 'ten cent' tour of Moscow, racing around the icy roads of Moscow's city centre. There was the obligatory visit to the Kremlin, followed by a trip to the new McDonalds burger bar, which was very nice, but most Muscovites couldn't afford to buy a 'Big Mac'. It all seemed a little sad to me. This was a proud nation which has, in the space of only a few years, been torn apart, both geographically and economically. If a couple of years ago we had told the Russian people that their major currency would change to the American dollar, they would have laughed at us. But here they were, in 1993, trading in US dollars with the value of the rouble falling almost to nothing.

On the flight back to London, Dave and I went over the

provisional plan set out by Dmitry. From Moscow we could charter an An-74 aircraft and fly to Chersky in Siberia, where we could then stay for about ten days in order to prepare our equipment and do some serious training. It had now been made Russian law that if aircraft wished to fly out over the Arctic ocean then, for reasons of safety, there must always be two aircraft. Therefore, from Chersky we needed to charter two An-2 aircraft to transport the expedition north to Henrietta Island, possibly via the now abandoned Russian polar station on Zhokohov Island in the New Siberian group. This plan sounded too simple to be true, and was one which in the end bore little resemblance to the final journey.

Back home the pace of life became more and more hectic; all three of us begged or borrowed a fax machine each and were then able to circulate updated progress reports instantly. Dave would fax through long lists of equipment with complex weight calculations, while I kept up negotiations with our Russian friends and equipment suppliers. In the meantime, Steve continued to commute between Burton and London for meetings with *The Guardian* or Save the Children, leaving a trail of spent telephone cards along the way. Packing cases full of expedition equipment started to arrive and I stored them all in my loft prior to being packed for air freight to Moscow. My wife Tracey very patiently put up with boxes of kit strewn about the house and being awakened at six in the morning by the fax machine receiving yet more information from our Russian friends. Slowly but surely, most of the main items of equipment had either been obtained or were ordered.

The Guardian ran an initial article outlining the basic objectives of the expedition, part of which covered the high-calorie diet which we intended to keep to during our time on the ice. One of the ingredients of our proposed diet was salami. The *Guardian* article went out throughout Europe, and one day Dave received a call from a man in Budapest. He said that he was interested to read that we would be taking salami and would we like him to send us some of the finest Hungarian salami to take with us. Very diplomatically, Dave accepted his very kind offer and thought no more about it until he received a letter from Manchester airport asking for a consignment of salami to be collected! As I lived closest to Manchester, I got the job of collecting it. My car still reeks of the stuff, but it was, without doubt, the best salami I have ever tasted.

Over the two-week Christmas period the expedition came to a grinding halt as companies closed down for the festive season. This was an exasperating time for all three of us, but it allowed me to spend some time with my sorely neglected wife and daughter.

The new year, 1994, started with a frenzy of activity. Certain items of equipment which were having to be specially made were behind schedule, which was not good, as it meant that should any fine tuning alterations be required we would just not have the time to carry them out before our planned departure date. Our list of supporters and sponsors was now growing daily. Most equipment suppliers we approached really did their best to help, even though almost all the companies we approached had already been the target of the Sir Ranulph Fiennes expedition machine. Paramo Clothing made all our outer shell clothing free of charge and this turned out to be without doubt the most functional, durable and comfortable shell clothing I have ever used.

Over the Christmas period, Dave had become increasingly worried about an old injury to his left knee, which was starting to cause him some trouble. He talked the problem over with Steve, who immediately arranged for him to have the knee operated on using keyhole surgery. Dave spent a day in hospital having his knee joint cleaned out, then travelled all the way home to Cumbria on the train, lugging with him a rucksack containing about a hundredweight of salami. Before this type of surgery became available, it would have meant a long stay in hospital, followed by around six months' rehabilitation.

As far as communications were concerned, this was left in the very capable hands of Laurence 'Flo' Howell, whom I first met in Antarctica in 1979 when he arrived at Rothera base to take over as radio operator. Flo now works for Philips Petroleum, but agreed to put together all our communications kit and act as our UK communication base from his home in Aberdeen. Flo had a huge one-hundred-and-fifty-foot scaffolding tower erected outside his house to carry the aerial system which would be required for radio communication with the expedition out on the ice. He also obtained for us, on loan, three 'SARBE' personal emergency beacons and a 'SARSAT/COSPAS' beacon which had fifteen pre-programmed messages, so should the radio malfunction or be lost we could still continue by using the beacon. The codes were:

Code 0   HF RADIO FAILED, CONTINUING ONWARDS, WILL SEND POSITION WITH SARSAT AS SCHED-ULED

1.   ALL OK, PROGRESS SLOW (1–5 NAUTICAL MILES)

2.   ALL OK, PROGRESS GOOD (6–10 NAUTICAL MILES)

3.   ALL OK, PROGRESS VERY GOOD (11 + NAUTICAL MILES)

4.   REQUIRE NON-EMERGENCY PICK-UP; CON-TACT BRADLEYS; WILL SARSAT/COSPAS POSI-TION DAILY; WILL ATTEMPT TO MOVE TO POSITION WHERE AIRCRAFT CAN LAND; WILL MONITOR CHANNEL 10 FOR AIRCRAFT AT 1900 UTC DAILY FOR ONE HOUR

5.   REQUIRE NON-EMERGENCY PICK-UP; CONTACT DMITRY SHPARO; WILL SARSAT/COSPAS POSI-TION DAILY; WILL ATTEMPT TO MOVE TO POSITION WHERE AIRCRAFT CAN LAND

6.   REQUIRE MEDICAL EVACUATION; CONTACT BRADLEYS; WILL SARSAT/COSPAS POSITION DAILY; WILL ATTEMPT TO MOVE TO POSITION WHERE AIRCRAFT CAN LAND; WILL MONITOR CHANNEL 10 FOR AIRCRAFT AT 1900 UTC DAILY FOR ONE HOUR

7.   REQUIRE MEDICAL EVACUATION; CONTACT

73

DMITRY SHPARO; WILL SARSAT/COSPAS POSITION DAILY; WILL ATTEMPT TO MOVE TO POSITION WHERE AIRCRAFT CAN LAND

8. STOPPED DUE TO LARGE OPEN LEADS, AWAITING REFREEZE OR CLOSURE

9. VERY HEAVY PRESSURE RIDGES MAKING PROGRESS SLOW; ALL OK

10. SLOW DUE TO HAVING TO NAVIGATE AROUND OPEN LEADS OR USING FLOATS TO CROSS

11. WE ARE MAKING SLOW PROGRESS TO THE EXTENT WHERE FOOD AND FUEL WILL NOT BE SUFFICIENT TO GET TO CANADA; WE PLAN TO STOP AT POLE

12. WE EXPECT TO ARRIVE ON THE CANADIAN COAST SOME FIVE DAYS FROM NOW; PREPARE BRADLEYS ETC.

13. DEEP SOFT SNOW CAUSING SLOW PROGRESS; ALL OK

14. HAVE FOUND NEWLY REFROZEN LEAD WHICH IS TRAVELLING IN THE RIGHT DIRECTION; MAKING GOOD PROGRESS

15. *SEARCH AND RESCUE*; WE NEED IMMEDIATE EVACUATION FROM THIS LOCATION, DUE TO INJURY; ONE 121.5/243MHZ PERSONAL BEACON HAS ALSO BEEN ACTIVATED; CONTACT L. HOWELL ASAP; RESCUE COULD COME FROM CIS, CANADA, OR CLOSEST RESCUE CENTRE

We hoped that these code messages would fit almost every eventuality, but as a last resort we had a personal emergency beacon set to the international distress frequency of 121.5/243 MHz. This, in theory, would bring help from the nearest search and rescue centre if needed.

To ensure that the expedition would stand the best chance of reasonable communications, Flo suggested that our field camp aerial should be raised to about twelve feet off the ground. At first we thought that we would have to design and engineer some sort of lightweight mast for this purpose, but then I had the simple idea of fitting a ski pole to the top of our tent, thus getting the required height and suspending the aerial from this.

Dave had been working hard over the last few weeks, sorting out the food. The manager of his local supermarket had become very suspicious of him as he strolled around his store with his notebook and pen, making notes of the nutritional information printed on the side of food packets. After much hard work, Dave and Steve announced the final diet. The main basic requirements of the diet had to be that it gave each expedition member the possibility of 6,050 calories per day and that the dry weight of this should not exceed one kilo per man per day. By fortifying much of the main bulk with vegetable suet the 6,050 calorie target was met. Together, Dave and Steve cooked up a formula for a very unique energy bar, which in itself packed 2,000 calories. Christened the 'Tweet' bar (due to the fact that before it was cooked, the dry ingredients bore a strong resemblance to bird food), this bar was made by mixing peanut butter with groundnuts, vegetable suet and many other goodies, boiling the mixture in a pan, then pouring it out on to trays to set. The cooled slab was then sliced up into bars and sealed in polythene bags. The whole thing tasted hideous, but later on during the journey itself we started to crave for them and quite often a full bar would be devoured in one sitting. Nestlés of Ashbourne donated about 400 large bars of 'Bianco' white chocolate with hazelnuts, which complemented our high-fat diet well, as according to Dave's nutritional research 'Bianco' had the highest fat content.

By the middle of January we were starting to panic more than a little. The sleeping bags that we had ordered had been manufactured wrongly and had to be done again. The sledges still hadn't arrived and neither had our boots, which were on their way from Canada. There was also the little job of packing all the food, fuel and equipment for freighting out to Moscow. Eventually, after many fraught telephone calls, all our equipment arrived and could now be made ready for packing. My loft now groaned under the weight of all this kit. We were now looking for a fourth man, who would act as a reserve in the event that one of us became injured or ill. Fortunately, an old friend of mine, Punch Wilson, agreed to take on this role. I had been to Baffin Island with Punch in 1990 and knew that he would be the perfect choice.

Dave drove down to Buxton and together we started to pack all the expedition equipment and food into packing cases, numbering each box and making box contents lists which were then immediately faxed to Dmitry in Moscow. Dmitry assured me that by having the box contents list he would be able to arrange its swift passage through Russian customs without any of the boxes having to be opened. All our fuel had been specially packed by Lloyds packagers of Manchester, who had done a very professional job. In total we had ten very large packing cases, three sledges and seven boxes containing eighty litres of paraffin and six litres of surgical spirit. Two weeks before our planned departure date, Dave and I finally loaded up all the expedition cargo into Dave's old camper-van and my car and delivered it to British Airways' world cargo office at Manchester airport. After about three hours, all our cargo had been X-rayed and checked in. The man at the counter looked confused as he handed back the paperwork and apologised to me for the time it took to sort out our cargo; 'but', he said, 'I've never processed a free one before.'

Firearms are a necessity in the Arctic, but only to be used as a last resort against an attack by a polar bear. Your first line of defence is to make loud noises and try to scare it away, and to this end we bought a quantity of quite large theatrical thunderflashes which I thought would do the job nicely. As for firearms, we decided against rifles mainly on account of their weight and opted for the only alternative weapon capable of stopping a polar bear, a .357 calibre Smith and Wesson Magnum handgun. I purchased two of these 'Dirty Harry' type weapons along with 100 rounds of soft-nose cartridges. Fortunately, we never had the need to use them, which was lucky, for when we returned to England after the expedition I found out that one of the guns was faulty and would hang fire when used.

On 28 January, a little over one week before our departure, a major problem regarding our firearms confronted us. I received this message from Dmitry:

> Dear Clive,
> Today we received a phone call from the Ministry of Internal Affairs of Russia and we were informed that a new law has been adopted that bans the import of firearms to Russia (with the exception of hunting and sporting weapons). Certainly this was a great surprise for us. Now we undertake all possible efforts (even addressing the Prime Minister), but maybe on Monday and Tuesday we can need your assistance.
> Sincerely yours,
> D. Shparo

This was indeed a major problem, as the expedition could not proceed to the Arctic without firearms. To set out to cross the Arctic ocean without protection against polar bear attack would be suicide. We talked over many alternatives and even discussed changing our starting point from Russia to Canada, and after much debate we could see no acceptable solution to the problem. At the next opportunity I made a telephone call to Dmitry, and told him that should it be impossible for us to take firearms across Russia, then the expedition would have no alternative but to reconsider its plan and change its starting point to a site on the Canadian side of the Arctic ocean.

Over the past few months I had got to know Dmitry quite well, and it had become very obvious to me that he had one enormous weakness – money. At this stage, we had not yet paid him the first instalment of his fee, so he knew that should he fail to obtain the necessary permissions for our firearms as set out in our contract with the Adventure Club, then we would change our plan and he would receive nothing. The following day the telephone rang; it was Dmitry: 'Clive, I now have all the permissions you need, including permission for your firearms. I will fax copies to you now.' We then sent him his cheque.

On 29 January, Tracey and I drove up to the Lake District where we met up with Steve, Dave and Dave's girlfriend Jane for a pre-expedition 'bash' at the Screes Hotel in Nether Wasdale. Flo and Morag Howell drove down from Aberdeen to join us along with many other mutual friends. Jane had very kindly organised musical entertainment by booking her favourite local blues band, which was actually two bands who had joined forces. One band had been called 'Slap the Dog' and the other 'The Last Chance', therefore, the joint product now went by the name of 'Last Chance to Slap the Dog'. The 'bash' went on into the early hours, with everyone drinking and dancing to the very limits of human endurance; I suspect some even went beyond that! Most people had very wisely booked rooms at the hotel, and it was a sad group of extremely pale faces who attended breakfast the next morning. I spent the last few days before departure at home with Tracey and Hannah. There were as always a few last minute things to sort out, but we were as ready as we could ever be.

On 6 February 1994 my father-in-law drove me down to Watford, where I met up with Punch. The two of us then drove down to his sister's house, which is reasonably close to Heathrow airport, where we stayed for the night. Next day, we met up with the rest of the team by the British Airways desk at Heathrow. Our bags were checked in, but the two Magnum handguns proved to be a bit of an eyebrow raiser! Eventually, all the formalities and paperwork were completed and we were allowed through to the departure lounge to await our flight to Moscow. Should everything be going to plan, our twenty boxes of expedition cargo should also have been loaded on to the same aircraft.

The flight to Moscow went smoothly and, after clearing passport control, we again met Sasha who gave us his usual hearty greetings. The guns again proved even more of an eyebrow raiser with the Russian customs, and it was only after the intervention of Sasha who had come armed with letters of authority from the chief of police that we were allowed to bring the guns out of the airport. Sasha took me to one side and said: 'From now on keep these weapons out of sight and do not even talk about them to anyone. We will only refer to them as "special cargo" from now on, OK.' I got the message; these weapons are now much sought after by the Moscow underworld and they would not be very particular about their methods for removing them from my possession. Meanwhile, Steve had managed to acquire a large quantity of champagne in small bottles and he, Dave, Punch and our reporter Tim Radford were busying themselves trying to drink as much of it as possible.

Our next port of call was the British Airways world cargo office, where we hoped to find out where our expedition cargo was being held so we could arrange for it to be transferred to the Adventure Club building. It was important that we collect the cargo that evening as we were booked on a military flight out of Moscow to Tiksi at eight the next morning. At the BA office, they knew nothing about our cargo. There followed a few frantic telephone calls to London and it was discovered that the cargo had not been loaded on to our flight. The reason was that Heathrow had something in the region of a 600-ton backlog and our expedition cargo had a low priority. I explained to the office manager that we were due to fly out to Siberia tomorrow and therefore would appreciate some kind of urgent action. We gave them the telephone number of the Adventure Club and asked them to contact us there as soon as they had some news.

At the Adventure Club we were greeted by Dmitry and treated to a banquet before being driven to the 'Sputnik', which is the Russian version of a youth hostel. I only managed a few hours' sleep as I had a suspicion that the beds we were sleeping in had other forms of wildlife living in them and they objected to me being there. Next morning we went back to the Adventure Club to await news of our expedition cargo. Punch rang the airport and was told that our cargo had now been loaded, but the flight from London was delayed. The plane finally landed at 6.35 p.m. Moscow time, and by that time the Moscow cargo office had closed. Dmitry made numerous telephone calls in an attempt to get the cargo office re-opened. I drove out to the airport with the club's driver in their minibus so we could be ready to pick up the cargo as soon as it could be released. We spent several very cold hours waiting by the airport gates, but nothing happened and we returned to the club. When I arrived there, supper was being served and we were introduced to Mitsuro Ohba, the man from Japan Dmitry had told me about. He was intending to travel to the North Pole solo, starting out from Cape Arctichesky at the northern tip of Severnya Semlaya. We were also introduced to Sergey, a member of the club who would be acting as our liaison officer as far as Henrietta Island. After supper we returned to the Sputnik.

At 9.30 a.m. I was woken by the telephone ringing. It was Sasha. 'Hello Clive, your cargo arrived at 3.00 a.m. and is now on its way to the military airport. You must have breakfast quickly and leave soon'. We caught a trolley bus over to the Adventure Club, where Dmitry had arranged for us to have breakfast. After breakfast Dmitry called me into his office and took our guns from his safe and handed them to me saying, 'Be careful with these and be sure to give them to the station officer at Tiksi.' Sergey had been listening to this and outside the office whispered, 'Forget that, just hide them.' Before we left the club, we all gathered in the club office to take part in an old Russian custom of a few moments' silence before we departed. We said goodbye to Tim, who was returning to London, and were then driven out to the airport, which was a hell of a long way outside the city. We arrived around 2 p.m., as take-off was planned for 3 p.m. The temperature at the airfield was about −20°C and, with no waiting room or shelter, we just stamped about on the runway to keep warm. It was interesting to see that although all the Russian military aircraft which were parked on the airfield were equipped with rear machine-gun turrets, most of the civilian transport planes also had rear turrets. Not all of them had guns in place, but all had the gun turrets as standard.

Finally the plane, an An-12 military transport aircraft, was ready for flying. We climbed aboard and sat in a small cabin situated just behind the flight deck. The plane was scheduled to take off at 3 p.m., but eventually took off at 6.30 p.m. We were soon to come to understand that in Russia, time management is an unknown skill. After take-off, Sasha opened up a large cardboard box and took from it some tins of corned beef and some bread; this was our in-flight catering. The door of our cabin was closed and the cabin pressurised as we reached cruising altitude. In the cargo bay the air temperature dropped to around −40°C, and some of the crew spent all the flight in the cargo bay.

After about four hours' flying, one of the crew members came into our cabin and said something in Russian which none of us could understand. This was then translated by Sasha, who said, 'We cannot fly to Tiksi today, the weather ahead is too bad. We are going to Engel's for the night, and if the weather improves we will continue tomorrow.' Engel's is situated on the banks of the Volga river, quite close to the border with Kazakhstan, once a highly secretive strategic air base and only half a mile from the spot where Yuri Gagarin, the first man into space, had landed on his return to Earth. During the Cold War, this would have been one of the major strike bases should Russia have decided to mount a nuclear attack on the United States or elsewhere. Huge bombers carrying nuclear payloads would have left this air base bound for targets in the USA. Their flight path would have taken them directly over the North Pole.

Once on the ground we were taken in a very crowded army personnel carrier from the airfield to the base and shown to rooms in a very basic looking military accommodation block. My priority was to have a shower and find something to eat, as it had been a long day. Sergey popped his head around the door and said, 'Have you still got the special cargo?' 'Yes,' I replied, pointing to my rucksack lying on the floor. 'Good, we will have supper soon.'

Not long after, Sergey returned, bringing with him some bread, tins of corned beef and some bottles of vodka. We decided to eat in the room which Dave and I were occupying, so Punch and Steve brought chairs from their room into ours. A little later Sasha arrived and with him was the pilot of our aircraft, who introduced himself as Alexis, and in turn we shook hands with him and then wished we hadn't. His hands were like shovels and had a grip like a vice. He turned out to be a Lieutenant-Colonel and a chief pilot in the Russian Air Force with twenty-four years' flying experience. Our gathering was quite unique: here we were, Westerners, sitting in a Russian strategic air base in middle Asia, drinking vodka with a high-ranking Russian officer. Three years ago this would have been impossible.

The following day, we were taken to the dining room for breakfast. The dining room was very large and elegant in design, with equally large Russian ladies serving up the food. Breakfast consisted of lamb with eggs and potatoes, bread, tea and cherry juice. The splendour of our surroundings made up for the poor quality of the food. We had some time to waste before our onward flight, so I took the opportunity to have a quick look around the base. To one side of the airfield I could see a large compound about the size of a football field on which stood countless helicopters, but on closer inspection I could see that all of them had parts missing. It would appear that they were being slowly cannibalised in order to keep others flying. Back at the accommodation block, Sasha announced that our plane was ready and that we should make our way to the airfield.

We walked the half mile back to the airfield and on the way passed lines of huge Russian bombers, covered in snow and unserviced. Looking at these sad looking but enormously powerful aircraft, which were built to deliver nuclear payloads, sitting in the snow really did confirm to me that the Cold War was definitely over. We all climbed back into the An-12, and to our amazement this time we had seven other passengers travelling with us and we all had to squeeze into the small cabin. Our cabin only measured two metres by three metres and now it had to hold thirteen people. Also onboard was a group of young and very scruffy-looking army conscripts, for whom I really felt sorry. They were made to travel in the cargo hold, which was unpressurised and unheated. Their clothes were old and certainly incapable of keeping them warm in the −40°C temperature of the cargo hold. After waiting for about an hour, the aircraft finally rumbled down the runway and clawed its overloaded frame into the air. Once in the air, one of the flight crew came back into our cabin and closed the small porthole in the door which connected our cabin with the cargo hold; the cabin was then pressurised, effectively sealing off our poor young army conscripts. All through the flight I could see them jogging about trying to keep warm, only occasionally being allowed, in turn, to have a few minutes in the warmth of our cabin.

After about two hours' flying, one of the crew came into our cabin and started to make coffee, but he only seemed to have three cups. It was a case of having to wait while three people finished their coffee, then he would make three more cups. When you finally got yours, it wasn't worth waiting for; strong, black and very sweet, but I was so thirsty by this time that I had to drink some of it. Like a magician, Sasha produced more bread and tins of meat from his cardboard box and we passed the time eating and looking over a map of the De Long Islands.

After five hours, we were on the ground once more, this time in a place whose name I could not get anybody to tell me. Whenever I asked, I just got the same reply: 'This is Bella Russia.' We worked out that we must be quite far north, but still a long way from Tiksi. From the airfield we were taken in what appeared to be an ex-army personnel carrier to a large but very run-down hotel, situated in a sort of small town. The temperature outside was very low and we were treated to a brilliant display of northern lights. The hotel was practically deserted, and because of our rather late arrival we had missed the evening meal. Sasha disappeared to see if he could organise something for us while we took our bags up to our rooms. By the time we returned to the reception area, Sasha as usual had worked his organisational magic and had arranged for a table to be set in the restaurant where we were served with a superb three-course meal followed by the now usual bottle of vodka. A 'happy evening' followed and we drank far too much vodka before staggering back to our rooms.

Morning started with Sasha knocking on our room door, saying; 'You must be on the bus in two minutes, no more.' We rushed around packing up our belongings and went down to the hotel reception. Outside, a military-style bus stood waiting, its exhaust forming large white clouds in the cold morning light. We were taken back to the airfield and dropped off at what can only be described as a briefing room. It had a huge globe of the world in one corner which measured about one and a half metres across, and on the walls were large maps of the north Siberian coast. The room was full of people, all waiting to fly out today. Punch wasn't feeling very well and sat down with his head on a table. Steve and Dave paced up and down impatiently and nobody seemed to know exactly what was happening. I was bursting to go to the toilet, so started searching for one and finally found it. It was a wooden shed outside, with a door that would not close, into which everyone of both sexes went to do whatever they had to do on the floor, where it just froze into solid piles.

After a very long wait, Alexis rushed in and gestured to us to go to the plane quickly. We almost ran across the frozen tarmac to the plane. After clambering up into the aircraft, we were followed by more and more people until there were twenty-four in our cabin, squashed in like sardines. Being first into the cabin, we had bagged the only seats. Steve sat in the corner and immediately went to sleep. Just before take-off, Sergey leaned over towards me and whispered the by now familiar words, 'Do you have the 'special' cargo with you?' I would just give him a confident nod in reply. Sergey would then break out into a broad grin, showing a full set of large white teeth. It felt like a scene from a Cold War spy thriller. The flight was hideously uncomfortable; we all had cramps and suffered from aching limbs. One man stood out from all the rest, in his very smart air force officer's greatcoat. He was a military doctor and spent most of the flight giving oxygen to some of the passengers. Halfway through the flight, Punch decided to start throwing up. Sergey found the waste bucket and passed it to Punch, who spent the rest of the flight with his head in it.

Five and a half hours later we put down in Tiksi. Climbing down from the plane on to the tarmac we knew we had arrived in Siberia. The temperature was about −35°C. Sasha shepherded us into a waiting army bus and we were taken to a very run-down apartment block, along with our 700 kg of expedition cargo. We were shown to rooms on the third floor and, before we knew it, all our boxes followed and were stacked in a spare room. This was supposed to be used as a base for our training period, but it was totally unsuitable for that purpose. It had been a long day, and thinking back I suppose I could have been more diplomatic, but at this stage I lost my temper with Sasha: 'How the hell do you think we can prepare and train for our expedition from the third floor in an apartment block in the centre of Tiksi?' Dave was far more relaxed about the situation, but even so expressed his dissatisfaction to Sasha. Steve just paced up and down, getting more and more annoyed at my harsh attack on Sasha. But we had travelled a long way and in my mind we deserved better service than this.

Later we were introduced to 'Major Sergey' of the Russian Army, who would be acting as our liaison officer with the chief of Tiksi, even though he spoke no English at all. Supper turned out to be more corned beef, but this time without the bread. While we sat and drank tea, we discussed the type of accommodation we would prefer to work from and, after this discussion, Sasha promised that he would endeavour to find a more suitable place in the morning.

The following morning, 12 February, Major Sergey arrived promptly at 9 a.m. He had obviously been practising a few words of English and as he came into our room he said 'Good morning, good morning, good morning' as he looked around the room. He escorted us through the apartment blocks, over snow drifts and into another block which looked just like all the rest. This was the local cafeteria where we were to have our breakfast. It consisted of rice, pasta and pork (I think) washed down with lots of Russia's most popular beverage, 'chigh' (tea). After breakfast, Major Sergey organised a rather rough-looking army half-track vehicle to transport us down to the river ice. This was the Lena Delta, where De Long and his men struggled to get to after the *Jeannette* had been crushed in the ice further north. The temperature was around −36°C, with a sharp wind which cut right through us as we walked along the river ice. Major Sergey showed us a building which was being used as a radio shack and suggested that we may be able to use part of this building for our preparations. It looked just about right for our purpose, so we agreed. Walking back to the vehicle was very painful on the face and most of us ended up with white patches of frostnip on our nose or cheeks. Major Sergey disappeared, saying that he would try to get permission for us to use the radio shack building.

Back at the apartment block Dave suggested that we should make a start and sort out some of our gear. Punch and Dave unpacked the sledges from their boxes and we started to prepare the runners. It was at this point that a man wearing slippers and a cheap looking blue tracksuit walked into our room. He started asking lots of silly questions, which were translated by Sasha. He was very critical about our sledges and in his opinion they were all wrong. After explaining our food to him, he replied by saying he thought it wasn't much good and we should take more honey. Dave looked at me as if to say, 'Who the hell is this prat?', and then we found out that the 'prat' was in fact the Chief of Tiksi and more than likely a member of the KGB! He then asked to take a look at my 'special cargo', and after doing a rather poor 'Dirty Harry' impersonation he shook his head and said that we should have brought a rifle. I can remember thinking, 'Well perhaps we should take more honey; then if the Magnum bullet doesn't stop a bear, we can always throw tins of honey at it!'

Later in the day, Sasha informed us that the Chief of Tiksi had invited us to partake of a Russian sauna and would be sending a car for us. Steve was feeling quite ill and stayed in bed all day, so when the car, which turned out to be a fur-lined jeep, turned up, Dave, Punch and myself went along. In the sauna, our host showed us round. We got undressed and went into the sauna room and all three of us sat on the lowest bench. Then in marched the Chief. He climbed up on to the top bench and started to throw more water on the stones. The heat was enough to boil your eyeballs and I am sure he was trying to kill us. Punch and Dave just sat there and the look on their faces said it all. Sweat was starting to gush from our skin, so much so that I thought my body was starting to shrink. Before long we could stand no more and made a dash for the door. It was a luxury to take a cold shower, but as we were just cooling off, the Chief returned with our chief pilot and insisted that we go to the steam for another session. Not wanting to offend him we returned to the heat. More and more water got thrown on to the stones until the thermometer on the wall reached about 120°C and I could not stand any more. We all piled out together, followed by the Chief, who then pointed to the door. Dave gave a disbelieving 'Oh no, not outside; it's minus thirty-six out there!' The door was opened and we were obliged to run out in the snow. 'Could the old heart stand it?' I thought. Our bodies were subjected to an instant 156°C change in temperature. The Chief then started to rub snow on his body and gestured that we do the same. Back inside, the torture did not cease. We were subjected to another frying in the steam room, before being allowed to take a shower, finished off with a rub down with snow. I think in future I will leave the old Russian customs to the old Russians.

After the torture session we all went into a lounge where we were served 'chigh'. On the table was a large ornate silver samovar, which was used to heat water. The hot water was then used to dilute strong concentrated tea which had been prepared in a separate teapot. The Chief was still insistent that we should take plenty of honey with us and was even using it to sweeten his tea. Refreshed by the sauna torture, we returned to the apartment and continued getting our equipment ready. This was to be our last night in a heated room, but sleep was difficult as nearly all the rooms were overheated.

The following morning, after the usual breakfast of meat, rice and tea, we moved all our equipment boxes down six flights of stairs to the front door of the apartment block and waited for the half-track. We waited and waited and at 10.30 a.m. It finally arrived. Major Sergey explained to us, via Sasha, that they had had difficulty in starting the vehicle and apologised for the delay. Our expedition cargo was quickly loaded on to the roof of the vehicle and we climbed into the back through a small hatch. We shot off towards the old radio shack at a great rate of knots, with spindrift billowing into our compartment through gaps in the sides.

When we arrived, we climbed out covered from head to foot in snow. The shack was already occupied by two quite young Russian soldiers from Yakutia, who looked rather bemused as we unloaded our boxes outside. Major Sergey showed us around some rooms inside the shack, which were perfect for our needs. We had one room to store prepared gear, one room to cook in, plenty of floor space for sleeping, and the use of the generator room to dry out kit. The two soldiers passed through occasionally; they smiled and nodded to us politely, but said nothing. We had decided to start sleeping outside to let our bodies get used to the cold, so Dave and I put our tent up in the small compound next to the shack.

We had a very warm and comfortable night in our double sleeping bags, in fact it was if anything too warm. The temperature overnight dropped to −43°C and our new, dry sleeping bags performed very well. Some fifty metres from the shack was the river ice of the Lena. Running along the shoreline was a large tide crack, which would be useful for training purposes. To start with, we loaded 120 kilos of gear on to the sledges and hauled them down on to the river ice for a trial run. To our amazement we found that we could actually move them and this even brought a smile to Steve's face, who was always the sceptic when it came to working out just how much we thought we could pull. Outside the temperature had warmed up to −36°C and we piled into our tent with only our single outer sleeping bags and a foil 'space bag' liner each. This seemed to be adequate and we all had a comfortable night's sleep. The next morning, we even discussed the idea of only taking the one sleeping bag, thus cutting down on weight. Punch came out to us with three mugs of tea, which we drank while planning the day's training.

After breakfast, the sledges were loaded up to 150 kg and we pulled them out on to the ice. They felt hellishly heavy and were hard work to pull, but we were all happy with the way they pulled over rough ground. While we were out on the river ice a light wind blew up, which gave us a chance to try out the parawings. Even with only a breath of wind, it assisted with the pulling and it was obvious that given the right set of circumstances they would prove to be very useful indeed. While we tested the parawings, Punch sat in the tent with our satellite navigator and succeeded in collecting an almanac from the satellites and initialised the instrument to our new location. This took quite some time to complete, and with the air temperature down to −40°C it made for a very uncomfortable job. Out on the ice, we had a few hiccups. While pulling over the tide crack ice, both Dave and I had bust the pulling points on the side of our 'Snowsled' harnesses. Steve had no such problem, as he had quite wisely decided to use the 'Troll' harness which he had used on his Greenland expedition. The rest day was spent in carrying out alterations to our harnesses and preparing the sledges. Steve decanted our fuel from the freight containers into thirteen five-litre containers, which we would be taking with us.

We had brought along quite a lot of spare sledging rations and for our evening meal we cooked some of this in an attempt to start absorbing the high-fat diet. We all gave the food a big thumbs up; even Sasha seemed to enjoy it. Sergey appeared from time to time, strutting about in his long fur-lined leather coat and jackboots. We decided to continue sleeping out with only one sleeping bag. Little did we know that tonight the temperature would fall to −45°C. Most of the night I shivered and both Steve and Dave admitted that they were very cold all night. It was decided there and then that we would take both our sleeping bags and, as things turned out, it would have been wise to have taken spare sleeping bags. The inside of our tent was just a mass of frost, and getting out of our bags needed a strong effort of will. Frost from the tent walls fell into your face and sleeping masks were frozen as hard as iron.

We made a quick exit from the tent and into the warmth of the radio shack, where Punch had by now prepared a hot breakfast. After breakfast, we had a photo shoot down by the tide crack. Punch took pictures of the three of us waving flags and banners, which showed the names of companies who had supported the project. The rest of the day was spent finalising our own personal gear. In the evening, Sasha arrived and told us that it may be possible to fly over to Chokurdakh, at around 8. a.m. tomorrow. All our gear was packed into the sledges ready for taking to the airport and all unnecessary kit was packed into a packing case which Punch was going to take back to England. With no tent to sleep in, we had the luxury of a warm night's sleep in the shack.

Sasha woke us at 5.30 a.m., and after breakfast we took the sledges outside to await the arrival of the truck. It was only just getting light when the vehicle finally arrived. Major Sergey walked into the shack and gave his usual 'Good morning, good morning, good morning' to everyone and we went outside to load up. The sledges were loaded and we all piled in on top of them.

The journey to the airport was an amazing experience. It was a bloody cold morning, but the sky had a strange, almost surreal quality about it. A faint pink glow sat close to the horizon, with the rest of the sky a deep purple. At the airfield, an An-12 stood waiting. The engines were running and there seemed to be the usual disorganised chaos going on, which we had by now come to expect. There was a powerful blast of hot air streaming out from the engine exhaust outlet and, to warm up, we took turns standing in the air stream.

This particular flight certainly ranked as the best one yet; it was only one and a half hours long, but it took us over some superb Siberian wilderness country. On arrival at Chokurdakh the sun was shining with an air temperature of only −27°C, and following our acclimatisation in Tiksi it felt very mild indeed. Our gear was unloaded and taken to the airport fire engine shed, which was about thirty yards away. Each sledge was carefully carried into the shed and placed on large sheets of cardboard to protect the runners. The truck then took us down the road to a small building, which turned out to be some sort of transit hotel occupied by some very odd people, and Sasha had arranged for us to stay here until we had the right weather conditions to fly north to Henrietta Island.

Once we had put all our bags into the rooms, Sasha took us to the local eating house where we were treated to reindeer burgers, with rice and, of course, lots of 'chigh'. After lunch, we took a constitutional walk around the settlement. Chokurdakh is only a small settlement, with a population of 6,000, mainly Yakut Indians. From the scant information which I gleaned from local people, it would appear that at any one time only 3,000 people actually live in the settlement. The other 3,000 live on the land outside the settlement.

Back at the hotel, Sasha brought news that the An-12 pilots would need to put in a depot of fuel on the New Siberian Islands and would be doing this tomorrow. Once the fuel was in place, then we could be flown to Henrietta Island as soon as weather conditions allowed. At this stage of the expedition this was no big deal, as we wanted some time to fine tune the packing of the sledges and, in any case, Chokurdakh was quite a nice place, so we occupied ourselves playing at tourists for a day or so. Unfortunately for me, I was struck down with a severe dose of the Siberian 'runs', spending most of this time locked in the bathroom, and in a country which seems to think that toilet paper is a luxury my personal laundry became rather disgusting. Sasha, as usual, tried his best to look after our welfare and organised a visit to the local natural history museum. This turned out to be a very interesting visit, with the local school mistress being employed to translate the museum curator's commentary.

Later we went to the post office, in the hope of buying postcards to send home. Luckily they did sell postcards of a sort and I asked the woman in the post office, 'How long will it take for a letter posted in Chokurdakh to get to London, England?' She replied, 'Oh . . . one month, two months, maybe never!' I took out a ten-dollar bill from my wallet to pay for some postcards and was immediately told by our schoolmistress to 'Put that away, it is a lot of money here!' It turned out that ten dollars is the equivalent of a month's wages in Chokurdakh.

We had our evening meal at the local eating house, and afterwards went to the house of the local schoolmistress, who had invited us for tea. Our hosts turned out to be five female school teachers, all from the local school, who were desperately trying to teach their pupils English. The problem is that even they themselves had never spoken to an English person face to face. The evening was spent eating, drinking and answering hundreds of questions about the English language. After several hours of questioning, we politely made our excuses and returned to the hotel. Here, Sergey decided that seeing as it may be our last evening together before flying to Henrietta Island, we should make a serious attempt to finish off all his remaining stock of vodka. I don't seem to be able to remember if we did or not!

HIGH-LATITUDE
DRIFTERS

'Let us probe the silent places, let us seek what luck betides us;
Let us journey to a lonely land I know,
There's a whisper on the night-wind, there's a star agleam
    to guide us,
And the wild is calling, calling – let us go.'
                                              – Robert W. Service

'We must go to airport now.' I looked up from my bed and saw
Sasha stood at the door. 'We must go quickly.' Steve
groaned, 'What time is it?', and from under a pile of blankets on
the other side of the room I heard Dave's voice'; 'Half past five
in the bloody morning.' With no time for breakfast, we packed
up our personal bags and staggered out into the frosty night
air. The airfield was only a couple of hundred yards away and
we were soon back indoors in the warmth of the fire engine
shed. Our three sledges were quickly loaded into the two tiny
An-2 biplanes which Sasha had chartered for this last leg of
our journey to Henrietta Island. We had saved large pieces of
cardboard from the packing cases and these were placed on the
floor of the aircraft to give some protection to the sledge runners,
before being strapped down ready for the flight.

At first sight, the An-2 biplanes look very dodgy indeed.
This is totally due to their biplane design, which gives you
the impression that they are old aircraft; but in actual fact they

are quite new. These aircraft have been the 'workhorses' of the Russian Arctic for many years, rather like the de Havilland Twin Otter has been in the western Arctic, but unlike the Twin Otter, which is quite a delicate design, the An-2 is built like a tank. Until very recently, the An-2 was in continuous demand as a means of re-supplying Russia's once numerous polar stations, but now all this has changed. Due to lack of funds, almost all Russia's polar stations, including those in Antarctica, have been closed down completely or mothballed. This has left the aviation companies redundant and they have been forced to seek alternative uses for their aircraft.

After the sledges had been loaded, it started to snow and we all retired to the airport building to await the decision of the chief pilot, as to whether we would fly today or not. We sat in a small, cramped, overheated office, which very soon became full of cigarette smoke. I was still feeling very washed out and run down, after my skirmish with the Siberian runs, giving me cause for concern about my physical condition. We waited and waited, until 7.00 a.m., when at last the chief pilot finally decided to fly. The two small planes were started-up and then in turn taxied out on to the runway. Soon both planes were airborne and turned on to a northerly heading. The noise from the huge single engine was almost deafening and I watched with interest as one of the flight crew sent out Morse code signals on a very ancient looking radio transmitter. It was still dark outside and, looking out through the window, all that could be seen were streams of snowflakes flashing through the eerie glow of the wing lights, along with the occasional flurry of sparks from the engine exhaust outlet.

Slowly, the southern sky started to come to life and brighten with a cold early morning glow. Below, the drift ice of the Arctic ocean gradually appeared as the daylight increased. What we saw was quite a disturbing sight to all of us: what should have been solid, unbroken winter sea ice, was a mass of fractured, young ice and large areas of open water. Wide open leads stretched out to the horizon and were in general orientated east to west. This did not bode well, and I could see a strange look of mild disappointment on Dave's face, as he peered out through the window.

The morning gloom, turned into a grey, gloomy, overcast day, but the pilots continued to fly north and I could only assume that they must have some good meteorological information which we didn't know about, and that they must know what they are doing. My main worry was not the dangers of flying in such conditions, but the fact that should we be unable to make it to Henrietta Island and have to return to Chokurdakh, we simply could not afford to charter the aircraft for another attempt. For now, though, the flight continued and I kept my fingers crossed.

Dave spent nearly all the flight glued to the window, only occasionally passing comment about the 'shit state' of the drift ice down below, and he was right. After many hours flying, the New Siberian Islands came into view on the horizon and we descended and overflew a very nondescript, featureless, permafrost island. These islands rise up out of the water during the winter, as the permafrost expands and sink back to just beneath the water surface in summer when the ice melts. Down on the sea ice, near to the eastern edge of the island, I could see quite clearly the small cache of fuel drums which had been placed there the day before. I watched as the first An-2 made a low pass over the depot and, as it passed over the drums, a smoke bomb was dropped on to the ice. A long tail of black smoke streamed out across the brilliant white of the snow-covered sea ice. I watched as the first An-2 circled around, then made its approach to land, floating down onto the ice as light as a feather. Then it was our turn to land. We circled around and our pilot put the plane down by the side of the first plane and only a few yards from the fuel depot. I can remember thinking, 'These buggers have obviously done this before.' Refuelling was soon under way, so while the aircrews got on with it, Sasha and myself went for a short stroll along the coast of the island. About fifty yards along the coast we came across the tracks of a polar bear and an Arctic fox. Sasha pointed to the tracks and said, 'There, you see, where the ice bear goes, then so follows the polar fox.' Arctic foxes are essentially the garbage collectors of the far north, natural scavengers, and it is common for them to follow bears around cleaning up any scraps which the bear leaves behind.

There was a shout from the aircraft that they were ready to go, so we hurried back. Soon the two aircraft were rumbling across the ice and we were airborne again. We were still heading north, flying over more of the New Siberian group of islands. After a short while, one of the flight crew pointed out of the port window saying 'Zhokohov, Zhokohov. We all peered out and there beneath us was the now abandoned Russian polar station on Zhokohov Island. It was a sprawling station with many buildings and communication aerials, but now it is abandoned due to lack of government funding. Once we had cleared the northern edge of the New Siberian islands, both planes changed their heading slightly to the north-east and on track for the De Long Islands.

We continued to fly over depressingly poor polar drift ice, with much open water about. After what seemed like forever, a small dark line appeared on the horizon. It had to be Henrietta Island. Things didn't look good down below: young, thin, freshly frozen sea ice with large areas of open water. The closer we got to Henrietta, the worse it got, until we were actually flying around the island itself. The two tiny planes buzzed around the island like insects compared with the vastness of wilderness around them. After making one complete circle of the island at low level, it became clear that at no single point could we see any safe route from the island on to reasonably good ice. Our original plan was to land on the island's ice cap and stay for a few days at the abandoned polar station situated on the north coast, before starting out across the ice. This would now seem out of the question, and both planes put down on the only decent ice floe about half a mile north of the island so we could have a discussion. Down on the ice, the chief pilot suggested that in his opinion the wisest course of action would be to continue flying to the north and drop the expedition off at the point where the ice begins to look safer. We all agreed with this, because if we were to stick to our original plan, it would almost certainly have resulted in the three of us becoming stranded on Henrietta Island, unable to start out.

The aircraft took off once more and swung round to the north. After only about six nautical miles, the ice improved slightly and we asked the pilot to put down where he could. By now the daylight was fading and surface contrast was very poor. We circled around and made one low pass over a reasonably large pan of ice. As we were making the pass, Dave pointed out a very large lead of open water running along the northern edge of the ice floe on to which, it would seem, our pilot had chosen to land. If this was to be our starting point, then we would have to cross this if we were to make any further progress north. The landing was as smooth as ever, and once down on the ice we started to unload the sledges, as by now the daylight was almost gone. Farewell photographs were quickly taken and flares were set off, followed by lots of back slapping and good wishes. We said goodbye to Punch, without whose help I don't think we would have got this far quite as smoothly. He now had to make his way back to the UK alone. At this point Sergey came over to us and whispered, 'Do not worry, we will send a signal to say that you have started out from the island.' Dave immediately said, 'No, no, no, don't do that; our start point is six nautical miles north of the island, you must be honest about that.' It was obvious that to Sergey this type of minor deception would have been acceptable, but to us it certainly was not.

Both planes quickly took off into the gloom, then each in turn made one low pass over our position, before turning south and into the distance. I stood in silence and watched the tiny planes fly away until they disappeared from view. The silence was deafening. A feeling of total and utter isolation grabbed at me as the final sounds of the aircraft engines faded to nothing. 'Well, we made it,' said Steve. 'Yes.' Dave stood quietly looking around and said, 'What a wild place!' Then Steve said, 'Well then, shall we get the tent up and have a brew?' 'That's a great idea.'

The modified Khyam instant erect tent was pitched in seconds and Steve volunteered to be 'inside man' for our first night on the ice and disappeared into the tent with the groundsheet. Dave and I then passed in the sleeping mats, followed by the sleeping bags, lamp, stove and pots bag. The radio aerial was strung out and the snow valance of the tent weighted down by using our food bags. Small snow blocks were cut and piled by the door ready to be melted for drinks and food, and finally the sledges were closed up for the night.

Camp 1 on 19 February 1994. 'What a wild place'.

Day two and we prepare to tackle the first of what will be countless pressure ridges ahead.

We would plan to have two rest stops each day, when we would have a hot drink and a bar of 'Tweet'. Each stop could only last a few minutes, before the cold started to eat into your bones and freeze the sweat on your skin.

When the wind blew from the south, we drifted north.

At last, the day we had been waiting for. With the wind from the south and reasonably good surfaces we make good use of the parawings.

Below: Steve in his favourite state.

Right: Our small high frequency radio, which we used to make contact with Flo Howell who was based in Aberdeen.

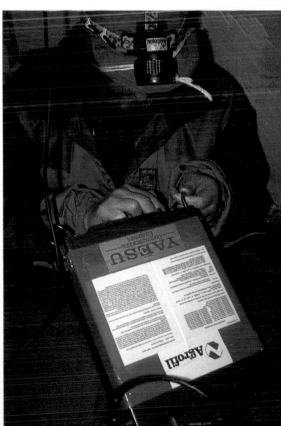

Ferrying.

A typical ridge, formed from broken young ice only about six inches thick.

Ferrying a sledge through broken ice.

A halt on the trail.

The first sign of older ice.

A stop for 'Horchoc'.

Home sweet home on the ice. Our Khyam instant erect tent was a godsend at the end of a long day.

Dave resting at the end of a long ferry leg.

Dave carrying the 'bear necessity' on his belt, inspecting a seal breathing hole in a freshly frozen lead.

Trying to get moving in the morning, after a painfully cold and sleepless night, demanded a great deal of willpower.

I knew that we had brought far too much ammunition for the 'special cargo', so this gave Steve the opportunity for a little target practice. After blasting off about fifty rounds of Magnum ammunition, even Steve, who said his eyesight was too bad to shoot straight, was now confident that should he be attacked by a polar bear it would die of severe lead poisoning in no time at all. With target practice over, Steve returned to his inside man duties, while Dave and I orientated the radio aerial on a compass bearing, aimed at Flo Howell's farmhouse in Aberdeen, Scotland. Before climbing into the tent I had a final look around in an attempt to absorb the surroundings a little. Our tent now looked minute against the awesome power and size of the icy wilderness in which it now stood. Our radio aerial looked quite impressive, stretched out above the tent to two ski poles either side of the tent, but would it work? Were Flo's calculations correct? A sudden cracking noise made me look to the north, where a large pressure ridge obscured the view. Just beyond this ridge lay a wide lead of open water which we had to cross if we were to make any further progress north at all.

Inside the tent, we settled into our first night on the ice. With all the planning, preparation and damned hard work needed to get the three of us into this position now well and truly behind us, it seemed that the expedition was already about ninety per cent over. All that was left to do was to drag three sledges loaded with four hundred and fifty kilograms of Arctic life support as many miles to the north as are physically possible each day. Steve had made a brew and had started to prepare the first evening meal. At this point in an expedition, things always feel a little awkward, when a smooth daily routine has not yet been established. It normally takes a few days for this to happen, with an even share of the routine tasks being taken on by each individual.

Before leaving the UK, Flo had sent us three 'Philips Petroleum' insulated mugs, which proved to be excellent. With an ordinary plastic mug, hot drinks have to be drunk almost immediately, otherwise, with the air temperature hovering around −50°C, they would be ice-cold in seconds. But with the Philips mugs this problem was overcome and we had time to enjoy our tea.

Later on, Dave tuned in our tiny high-frequency radio for the first time and at 7 p.m. local time he gave Flo a call: 'Mintlaw radio, Mintlaw radio, Mintlaw radio, this is Zulu Zero, Zulu Zero, Zulu Zero, do you copy – over?' Dave repeated this call several more times. Then, to our amazement and sheer disbelief, we heard Flo's voice coming through loud and clear: 'Zulu Zero, Zulu Zero, Mintlaw radio, Mintlaw radio, one, two, three, four, five, five, four, three, two, one, this is Mintlaw radio; hello guys, good to hear you.' This radio contact was quite amazing and a great morale boost for our first night on the ice. I just could not believe that with such a small box of electronics we could be talking to Flo in Aberdeen. Earlier I had taken a position fix using the G.P.S. (Global Positioning System) satellite navigator, which had given our present position to be 77°17'N, 156°53'E – very close to the spot where the *Jeannette* sank over one hundred years ago. Dave passed this position fix to Flo along with our best wishes to our respective families. As tomorrow was Tracey's birthday, I took the opportunity to ask if Flo would pass on a few of my special thoughts to her by telephone.

Everything seemed to be going to plan and we all felt that this was a good start to the expedition. We had been unable to start from Henrietta Island itself, but we were happy in the knowledge that our starting position was the best that anyone could have done, taking into consideration the ice conditions that we had encountered this year. Perhaps in other years things might be different; in fact, in 1978 when Dmitry Shparo and his team left Henrietta Island, the ice was better and that was on 20 March. Here we were a full month earlier in the season, facing diabolical ice conditions, when logically the conditions should have been a lot better. Henrietta Island filled our southern horizon, and it was possible to pick out the small huts of the abandoned Soviet polar station perched on a level area above the ice cliffs. We tried to work out just how far north we would have to travel before the island disappeared below the horizon and out of sight, but in polar conditions it is hard to judge.

As we crawled into our sleeping bags for our first night on the ice, the outside temperature dropped to −30°C. Inside the tent, with our stove pumped up to full power, the temperature could be raised to about −20°C, but as soon as the stove was turned off, the temperature almost instantly plummeted to equal that outside. During the night, Dave and Steve got their first experience of ice noise and movement. Throughout the night the ice bumped and cracked, strange creaking noises came from under our tent, and occasionally I could hear the clatter of ice blocks falling from the pressure ridges which surrounded our ice floe. We all accepted that the surface across which we would be travelling was only a dangerously thin scum of ice floating on top of cold black water many thousands of fathoms deep, and to make things worse the thin scum of ice was being continuously broken up by the action of surface winds, thus increasing our already long list of objective dangers. I tried to put all the dangers to the back of my mind in an attempt to sleep, but it was almost impossible. Finally, through sheer exhaustion, I dropped off to sleep, but only for a short time before the cold which was striking up from the ice through two layers of foam sleeping mat eventually forced me to turn over. As I turned over, I could feel super cool air being sucked into my sleeping bag due to the 'bellows effect' of my body forcing warm air out. I shivered for a short while until the air inside my sleeping bag warmed up once more, then dozed again, and so it went on through the night.

Day two dawned grey and overcast. Steve, displaying a superhuman force of will power, had reached out from his sleeping bag and lit the stove ready for breakfast. Just the sound of the stove purring away gave me a psychological boost and a sense of warmth, although the temperature inside the tent still hovered around −35°C. Soon Steve passed over two 'Philips' mugs of instant tea. To drink the tea meant that you had to reach out one arm from your sleeping bag into the supercooled air outside. This is a very unpleasant process, requiring a strong effort of will. Firstly, the hood of your sleeping bag had become encrusted in a thick mass of ice formed from your breath freezing during the night, and this had to be cracked open. As the bag opens, clouds of vapour billow out and supercooled air is sucked in, chilling off your damp clothing. In an attempt to stop body vapour entering the sleeping bags, we used a vapour barrier lining bag, but this meant that your clothing became wet instead.

Soon, bowls of high-calorie breakfast cereal with hot milk were being passed around and this was followed by more mugs of tea. Steam from the food filled the tent to such a density that it became impossible to see each other across the tent. While eating breakfast, Dave very casually said, 'You know, chaps, the inside of my sleeping bag is very damp.' This in fact was very serious. If body vapour was getting into our sleeping bags it would freeze and slowly fill up the bag with ice. The result of this is twofold: firstly, the build-up of ice reduces the insulating quality of the bag; and secondly, the weight of the bag, which you then have to haul across the ice each day, is increased. During our training period at Tiksi, we had suspected that the vapour barrier inner linings of our sleeping bags were not totally vapour-proof, and to try and overcome this problem we had added an extra silver foil reflective 'space bag' liner, which we hoped would cure the problem and would also reflect back some of our body heat. But it was obvious that somehow this was not working and vapour was still penetrating through the barriers to form condensation on the inside of our sleeping bags. If this continued, we calculated that our sleeping bag units would become almost useless within a week. In these temperatures and without the insulation of a dry sleeping bag, we would easily freeze to death during the night.

Outside, visibility was poor, surface contrast was non-existent and our thermometer showed −38°C. In these conditions it becomes impossible to detect changes in surface undulations, with even large surface drifts (sastrugi) just blending into the overall whiteness and appearing as smooth, flat ice which can only be detected by stumbling into them. We made the decision to move north from our present position and at least try and get to the other side of the lead to our north.

After breakfast, we pushed through the tent door and out into the dim Arctic winter light. Dave and I started to pack up the sledges while Steve packed up the cooking stove and pots. The idea is that by the time the inside man has packed up, the only thing left to do is to collapse the tent, pack it on to a sledge, and you are ready to go. We just about managed this when Steve emerged from the tent and announced that before he could walk to the North Pole, he had one very serious task to perform, then strolled off into the distance clutching a toilet roll. As he walked away from the tent, he suddenly turned around and shouted, – 'Hey, come and have a look at this.' I walked over to where he was standing and was horrified to see that some time during the night our ice floe had split. A crack about a foot wide ran from the edge of the floe in a straight line towards our tent; then, about ten feet from the tent the crack had for some strange reason changed direction and shot off to the south. A good start, I thought, someone up there must be looking after us.

It is unbelievable the amount of time it takes to complete simple tasks. With numb hands, every job becomes a complex problem moving in slow motion and seems to take for ever to complete, sometimes requiring two of you to do it. After around two hours, we were ready to move off and made the decision to try and pull our individual sledges for a day and see how it goes.

It had snowed during the night and a light dusting of fresh powder snow had been blown over the ice. As I clipped on my hauling harness for the first time in anger, my mind filled with a strange but curious fear of what lay ahead for all three of us. We were well equipped and had a wealth of experience in polar travel, but out here you need a strong element of luck to go with it and without that the Arctic will simply stop you in your tracks, play with you for a while, chew you up and spit you out. We all accepted this risk, otherwise we would not be here. It was a gamble. We hauled away from the campsite, each of us curious as to how far we could pull these 150-kilo sledges, each of us silent in our own thoughts of what the future would hold. The wind had blown the fresh snow about, forming low mounds and hummocks with areas of bare ice in between. Hauling over the bare ice was an effortless doddle, but as soon as the sledges ran into the powder snow mounds the sweat started to squirt. It was like trying to pull the sledges through treacle, and it was made even more difficult by the absence of surface contrast. We were regularly walking straight into three-foot-high drifts with no indication that they were there. All surface features just blended into one complete whiteness.

The three of us stumbled on in a roughly north-easterly direction, until the pressure ridge which ran along the northern edge of our ice floe loomed ghost-like out of the grey gloom. We turned to the east and followed the edge of the ridge until, after only a few hundred yards, we came across an area of low rubble where it was possible to cross. Here it became obvious that we didn't stand a cat in hell's chance of pulling the sledges over this rubble alone and would start a routine of relaying which was to become a very familiar activity in the days and weeks to come. The hauling lines were adjusted and together we hauled the first sledge into the rubble. Pulling a dead load of around 150 kilos over ice blocks can be a very dangerous occupation. It would be very easy to break a leg or be crushed by an unstable ice block.

At long last all three loads were heaved over to the opposite side of the ridge, where we stopped for a short rest. We were now at the edge of the lead which only yesterday had been open water. Now we were looking at a broad strip of new ice about twenty yards wide, covered in large white frost flowers. I leaned over and tested the ice by jabbing at it with my ski pole and it seemed solid enough, so I thought I would try it out with the ultimate test and hauled a fully loaded sledge out on to it. Pulling a heavy sledge out on to thin ice is without doubt the best laxative known to man, and as I moved out into the middle of the lead the ice surface changed from white with frost flowers, to grey, greasy looking stuff which wobbled as I ski'd over it. Once on the far bank, I stopped to rest and wait for Steve and Dave to come across.

It soon became clear to all three of us that we would have to resort to relaying the sledges, as the weights were crippling to pull alone. We had all taken the wise precaution of wearing both knee and back supports to guard against strain injury, but the risk of a more serious injury was not worth our while. Dave suggested that we should rearrange the loads so that half the total weight was loaded onto one sledge and the other half would be split evenly between the other two sledges. The plan was that all three of us would haul the single sledge for about one mile, then we would return and haul the other two sledges connected in tandem along the trail made by the first sledge. This made the hauling much less of a strain. However, the disadvantage was that we had to walk three miles in order to make one mile of progress north. This also did not take into account the many extra miles which we had to cover when scouting out the route through pressure ridges, prior to hauling the sledges up the trail.

We continued with our relaying method for the rest of the day, with only one short stop at around midday for a hot drink of 'Horchoc' (a mixture of Horlicks and drinking chocolate) from our Coleman flasks and some 'Tweet' bar. By 2.30 p.m., the daylight was fast fading and so were we. Exhausted, we called a halt for the day with only two miles' progress to show for all our sweat and toil. While we were making camp, the wind which had been light and northerly all day began to increase. Dave cooked up our evening meal, during which the stove decided to explode into flames which rose dangerously into the roof of the tent. Total disaster was only averted by Dave's quick thinking, when he grabbed the largest pan and dropped it over the entire stove killing the flames in an instant. Serving out the food was another hazardous procedure, because as soon as the lid comes off the cooking pot the tent instantly fills with a dense fog of steam. The next thing you see is a plate of food which appears like magic through the gloom, and as it is impossible to see who's holding it you just say 'thanks mate' and settle down to eat. Next, a hand holding a mug of hot tea appears. You take the tea and replace it with your empty plate; the hand and plate then disappear back into the fog. It is quite some time before the fog clears and you are able to have a conversation with the others. Steve handed out the first of our anti-inflammatory pills which we had agreed to take as a preventative measure during these early days, when the sledge loads were at their heaviest. Before turning in for the night, I took a position fix with the GPS, which to our dismay put us only .2 of a nautical mile further north of our last position. We were drifting south.

Day three started in silence. The wind which had increased in strength and buffeted our little tent all night had died away to calm; even the ice was silent. I lay in my sleeping bag wondering what today would bring and trying to bring life back into the tip of my nose which had become frostnipped during the night. Soon there was movement from Dave's sleeping bag and a frost-covered head and one hand emerged, followed by a cloud of body vapour. I could hear him trying to coax a cigarette lighter to work: 'Oh, come on, light you little . . .' After some time the lighter sparked into life and he reached over to the stove which he had meticulously prepared last night. The spirit bowl had been filled and a small piece of J-cloth placed in the bowl to act as a wick and help to light the spirit. Once the J-cloth had warmed up the spirit enough to make it burn, Dave slid back into the warmth of his sleeping bag to wait for the stove burner to become hot enough to work. In a few minutes Dave's hand appeared again; it reached over and turned the control knob on the side of the stove. After a short splutter of flames, the stove came to life with a pleasant purring sound.

Once the stove is going, the temperature inside the tent slowly rises bringing the dreaded moment when you have to get out of your sleeping bag ever closer. It was 'pee bottle' time. Dave, being the smallest of the three, somehow was able to use his pee bottle inside his sleeping bag. He would stopper up the bottle and keep it inside his bag where it would remain liquid, until morning when he would then pour it away. However, Steve and I, being much taller and wider in build than Dave, didn't have enough room in our sleeping bags to carry out this tricky manoeuvre safely. This meant that we were forced to get out of our bags during the night to use the bottle, or alternatively, try to put it out of our minds and wait until morning.

After breakfast, we packed our sledges and prepared ourselves for a hard day ahead. Just as we were about to leave the campsite, the sun peeped over the horizon bathing the surrounding icescape in a beautiful pastel pink light. As the day wore on, the sun made a low shallow arc above the southern horizon and the air temperature rose to around −20°C, which was a great boost to our morale. Deep soft snow covering broken ice made the going a strenuous task. Relaying our three loads over never-ending pressure ice. One hundred yards at a time and covering all gained ground three times. Dave and I frequently climbed to the top of high ridges in an attempt to pick out the line of least resistance through the chaos of ice which now surrounded us as far as the eye could see. From the tops of these ridges we just stood and stared in disbelief at the icescape which stretched out before us. No easy routes, just a chaotic mass of jumbled pressure ridges. Some years ago, a Canadian friend of mine had given me his description of the Arctic ocean and I could hear his words echoing around in my mind: 'Sledging on the Arctic ocean is rather like a child trying to ride its bicycle through New York city after it has been hit by a nuclear bomb.' Sometimes we would have a 'good' relay and cover about a hundred yards or so, but mostly it would only be a few yards to the next pressure ridge. The difficulties were relentless and it required every single ounce of our strength and will power to heave our three life support systems over each obstacle. Relay followed relay, until late afternoon, when we were stopped by open water and forced to camp.

The thermometer read −25°C, but it felt much colder as we put up the tent and I crawled in with the groundsheet to take my turn as 'inside man'. While the evening meal was cooking, I managed to get a GPS fix which placed us only one nautical mile north of our last fix. Talk about depressing; all we seemed to be doing was slogging our guts out each day just to stand still against the southerly drift of the ice. We fully understood that we would have to travel a long way north before we could hope to see any advantage from the trans-polar drift stream, but at that rate we would never reach it.

We sat and talked as we ate our high-fat meal. The food was still taking quite a lot of getting used to, but it was definitely an effective diet. After finishing his meal, Dave passed me his empty plate and said, 'Cheer up, it's pasta on day ten!' The rest of the evening was spent writing up our diaries and swapping stories while our SARSAT/COSPAS beacon sent out its Code 9 signal which we could only hope was being received.

Day four dawned fine and a warm pink glow filled the tent. After cracking open the hood of my sleeping bag, I reached out one hand and lit the stove. Before long the stove was purring away and I passed over two mugs of hot tea to Dave and Steve.

The temperature outside had dropped to −30°C and it certainly felt it. A smooth 'breaking camp' routine had now set in and we were ready to go by 11 a.m. As we started out hauling our first relay load of the day, the sun appeared on the horizon, forming a superb solar pillar of deep red light which dominated the southern sky. It was still only 22 February and at this latitude we could only expect about five hours of weak sunlight.

Pressure ridge followed pressure ridge, followed by rubble ice, followed by more high pressure ice. For about three hours we relayed the sledges through this mad labyrinth of broken ice. We stopped for a drink and to take stock of our situation. The ice all around was in motion, great cracks could be seen scything through the whole area. We were travelling over very young first-year sea ice, which was obviously absorbing massive pressure from the main polar drift ice far to our north. This was not good and was slowing down our progress to a crawl. Combine this with the strong, persistent southerly drift which we were encountering and we could even cancel out the crawl; we were just about standing still.

After we had had our drinks, Dave went on ahead to see what lay beyond the next ridge. He disappeared over the crest of a big ridge and a short while later appeared again and jogged back across the ice towards us. As he got closer, I could see a big grin on his face and Steve said, 'How's it look?' 'It's the dog's bollocks mate. . .just beyond this big ridge is a smooth pan of ice.' All three sledges were hauled over to the ridge and one at a time were relayed over to the other side. On the opposite side of the ridge was a short rubble field through which we coaxed the loads. Our sledges were made from Kevlar and were extremely strong, but the battering they were getting in this rough ice was leaving its mark on them. Large chunks of the outside gel-coat were being smashed off and we were leaving a green trail through the ice, as pieces of the green vinyl Carlsberg logo's were ground off by the ice. Once through the rubble ice, we hauled the sledges around a small ridge and slid out on to smooth ice. Dave was right, it was a large pan all right; you could see the ridges at the sides of the pan, but you could not see the far side. At last we could travel more than just a few yards at a time. We sorted out the hauling lines and set off like three carthorses pulling Dave's sledge. It was a real pleasure to get into a rhythm and stride out on smooth ice.

After about half a mile, the weather suddenly started to change. Thick cloud descended and a stinging wind blew up from nowhere. When I turned around I could not see the other two sledges which we had left at the edge of the pan. We quickly unhooked ourselves from the sledge and started skiing back, trying to follow our outward tracks, but these were slowly being obliterated by the wind. The situation was potentially disastrous. Should we fail to locate the other two sledges, we would become lost in the white-out with absolutely no chance of survival. With this unacceptable outcome buzzing about in my mind, I turned around and was just able to see Dave's sledge through the mank. I quickly took a compass bearing on the sledge, added 180 degrees and then continued on this bearing until the 'day-glo' orange sledge covers appeared through the whiteness like two beacons of orange light. The wind was getting stronger and our tracks had been wiped out. We soon set off hauling the two sledges back along the compass bearing I had taken earlier. About halfway back along the trail, the murk and wind started to lift and disappeared almost as quickly as it had descended.

We camped up very pleased with our day's efforts, and with the hope of better sledging to come our spirits were very high indeed. Later in the evening we were discussing our progress when Steve said, 'You know, the best thing about this fresh powder snow is that it covers up all the cracks in the ice and I like that.' He then went on to relate the story of a meeting with our expedition patron Sir Vivian Fuchs some time ago. Sir Vivian had quietly listened while Steve presented the expedition plan, to him and when Steve had finished he said, 'Now let me get this straight. You studied geography, then you became a yachtsman before going to Antarctica as a boatman, am I right? You then went to university to study medicine, after which you

107

crossed the Greenland ice cap. Now you plan to cross the Arctic ocean?'

'Yes that's right.'

'I like that.'

Just before we turned in for the night, the wind got up again and before long a full gale was blowing, making sleep difficult. The gale moaned throughout the night, gusting to around fifty knots and carrying with it much drifting snow. Our small lightweight tent stood up to the battering very well, even though we were in a very exposed position pitched in the middle of a large flat pan of ice.

Day five came round after a sleepless night, with the wind showing little sign of easing in strength. We were pinned down and unable to move. What did interest us, though, was the wind direction, which had veered round to the south. While breakfast was cooking, I managed to get a GPS position fix, which to our joy and total amazement showed an overnight drift of a full six nautical miles to the north! Throughout the day I took several more position fixes and by the end of the day we had drifted a further three nautical miles north. We joked at the possibility of the wind blowing as strong as this for the next ninety days, with the resulting drift transporting us to the Pole without the need to take another step! We were happy to send out a Code 2 on the SARSAT/COSPAS beacon even though we had been given a lift by the elements, but were unable to make contact with Flo at the pre-arranged time and decided to try him again in the morning. Outside the gale continued to moan past our tent, piling snow up around us. Spindrift blew into the tent through the smallest of gaps and covered our sleeping bags in a fine white layer. The condition of our sleeping bags was now giving us great cause for concern. Regardless of all our efforts to stop body moisture getting into the down, moisture was still getting through. My bag seemed to be the worst and Dave's was not much better.

The wind continued into day six, giving yet another sleepless night, but at least we were still being blown in a northerly direction, or to be more precise a north-easterly direction. We all stayed in our sleeping bags until about 10.30 a.m., when a strong call of nature moved me into action and Dave decided that it was time to have breakfast. With toilet roll in hand, I crawled through the tent door and out into the blowing gale. I noticed that during the night our radio aerial had blown down, but it didn't seem worth putting it back up again, as we really didn't have much progress to report. The most noticeable change was the air temperature which was dropping, and now the thermometer read −38°C.

Back inside the tent, breakfast was well underway and our radio had been tuned into the BBC World Service for an update on the world news and current affairs. It is at times of forced inactivity like this, that you often wish it were possible just to switch off your brain and move into a sort of standby mode, until the time comes when you need to think again. But as this is not possible, you can only sit or lie in your sleeping bag, with your own thoughts swimming around in your head. Time crawls by, punctuated only by meals, drinks of tea, short conversations and of course the BBC news broadcasts. It is a strange state of limbo which must be accepted, under the total control of the elements which will tell you when to switch back on again and start working.

Day seven turned out to be an important and quite eventful day. Firstly, the gale had died away overnight and amazingly the day promised to be fine but much colder. Secondly, because I had had precious little sleep over the last couple of days, I had, out of sheer exhaustion slept like the proverbial log and felt much better for it. Feeling refreshed after the first good night's sleep in a week, I packed up the sledges with a renewed enthusiasm. Thirdly, a weak but steady breeze from the south-south-west and smooth ice up ahead gave us our first real opportunity to try out the parawings.

Even though we had tried out the parawings in the UK and in Tiksi, it was still a skill which we needed to perfect and it looked as if we would have plenty of opportunity today. Once inflated, the parawings' pulling power is tremendous and it takes all your strength just to hold it back. If you fly the wing up above your head, it almost lifts you off the ice, and as you lower it to fly in front of you at about thirty or forty degrees above the ice, the full pulling power can be used to haul a sledge. At first we just clipped the parawing straight into the front of our hauling harnesses. This was OK for a while, until the constricting effect of the harness made it difficult to breath. After many trials we settled on a system where the parawing was linked directly to the sledge hauling line, giving the effect of a second person pulling the sledge. When the wind strength increased, it was possible just to ski along by the side of the sledge allowing the parawing to do all the work, only occasionally assisting it when the sledge hit mounds of sastrugi.

Setting out from our campsite with all three parawings flying was a great sight and added extra colour to our white surroundings which I could not resist capturing on film. The air temperature had plummeted overnight to −45°C, and with the wind chill factor added, it made travelling very uncomfortable. Throughout the day I stopped frequently to take photographs of Steve and Dave as they sailed towards me across the ice, with their parawings flying in a blaze of colour. It was a wonderful sight. Taking photographs also meant taking off my big outer gloves and consequently my hands got very cold and painful, but to get the pictures it seemed worth it. Later on the pain disappeared and my fingers just felt wooden. By midday, I realised that the feeling in my fingers hadn't returned from my last bout of photography, so I took my gloves off to check my hands. The fingers of both my hands were white and frozen, but I was confident that if I kept the fingers moving, they would eventually warm up and all would be well.

We were making good progress over reasonably smooth ice, but it wasn't long before we sailed back into broken ice again. At a narrow lead of open water I stopped and after collapsing the parawing took a walk along the edge of the lead to find a possible crossing point. Eventually, I came to a narrow spot with a loose ice block jammed across the lead which could possibly be used as a stepping stone. By the time I got back to the sledge, Steve and Dave had arrived and we all 'tacked' against the wind along the edge of the lead to the crossing point. With the assistance of the parawing, I got a good speed up before stepping out on to the loose ice block. As my weight came on to the block it sank slightly, but my momentum carried me over. The sledge followed and I hauled it away from the edge of the lead ready for the others to cross. Steve came next, with his parawing flying at full pelt. With all this physical exertion, Steve's glasses had become completely frosted over and he missed the crossing point by about a yard heading for open water. By this time he had gathered so much speed that it was impossible to stop and he stepped straight out over the inky black water. As his foot came down into the water, the wind gusted and Steve held onto the parawing control bar which held him up out of the water and then dropped him onto the opposite bank of the lead. The sledge followed, dipping into the water across the lead and bouncing up again onto the ice. Had he not had the assistance of the wind, Steve would certainly have been in for a good soaking. Dave had been watching this and quite wisely collapsed his parawing and hauled his sledge to the crossing point before stepping over.

By the end of the day, life had still not returned to my fingers and I was starting to become worried. After camping up, I jogged around outside the tent for a while and finished cutting snow blocks to be melted for water before crawling into the tent. Inside, Steve had a brew of tea ready which he handed to me. While we were drinking our tea, I removed my gloves to check my fingers. I was horrified to see that the ends of eight of my fingers were pure white and severely frostbitten. As the fingers thawed out in the warmth from the stove, the pain increased. My thoughts drifted back to 1985 and to the excruciating pain which I had gone through while thawing out my frozen feet. In 1985 I had been alone, but this time I was fortunate that there was a doctor in our party who had brought with him some strong pain killers which he gave to me, and this helped quite a bit. Steve also gave me a drug which is normally given to people suffering from angina. The effect of this drug was to dilate the blood vessels in the body's extremities, which in a case of frostbite would be very useful to help recovery. Even after painkillers, the pain in my hands continued to increase. Steve gave me more painkillers which helped a little but sleep was impossible. Dave had checked the thermometer earlier and was shocked to find that all the fluid in the thermometer had shrunk into the thermometer bulb. The last mark on the scale read -45° C, so we could only guess that the temperature must be -50° C at best, but we suspected that it was closer to -55° C.

111

The night which followed was unpleasantly cold. All three of us shivered the night away, even though we were sleeping fully clothed inside our double sleeping bags, complete with a reflective foil 'space bag' inner lining. To make things worse, our GPS navigator told us that we had started to drift to the south once more.

We had an early start on day eight, when Steve rose early and made a brew of steaming tea in an attempt to thaw us all out. It had been the coldest night yet and we had all suffered from lack of sleep due to the painful, penetrating cold. The cold would first of all enter your hip making the joint painful, but to turn over meant losing warm air from your sleeping bag which would be instantly replaced by minus fifty-five degree air from outside. Apart from the loss of heat from your sleeping bag, rolling over also caused a cascade of frost crystals to fall from the tent walls onto your face and onto other tent occupants, which in these circumstances is downright antisocial! Steve had lit the small paraffin lamp and hung it up in the middle of the tent. This produced a pleasant light and gave a comforting sense of apparent warmth. Dave tuned in our radio in an attempt to make contact with Flo. Since our first contact with Flo, we had not been able to make any further two-way contact. We had often heard Flo loud and clear, but unfortunately, he could not receive our transmissions. On each radio schedule Flo resorted to asking questions, which we answered by using the tuning signal – one beep for 'yes' and two beeps for 'no'. He also kept us informed of the results of our SARSAT/COSPAS beacon transmissions.

Dave sat by the radio holding the handset: 'Come on Flo, speak to us.' The radio just replied with atmospheric crackle, but a human voice faded in through the hum and crackle; it was Flo: 'Zulu Zero, Zulu Zero, Mintlaw radio, one, two three, four, five, five, four, three, two, one, Zulu Zero, Zulu Zero, Mintlaw radio listening out.' Dave gave a reply and waited and waited, only to be frustrated when Flo came back and said: 'Zulu Zero, Zulu Zero, nothing heard at this time, nothing heard at this time, I think it's get your boots on time, could you adjust your aerial and go down to channel ten?' We had been so used to this over the past week or so, that whenever Flo asked us to go outside and adjust the aerial, we would just tune to the required channel leaving the aerial as it was. Not to have radio contact for a night was far more preferable than getting out of your sleeping bag to go out into a raging blizzard to adjust the aerial.

After breakfast we pulled on our frozen boots and gloves and went outside to load up the sledges ready for another day of hard labour. The wind had died down somewhat, but our thermometer was still reading off the scale. Outside the tent, the first thing we did was jog around for a while trying to coax some blood into frozen toes and fingers. Steve came over to me and said: 'How's your hands?'

'Painful as Hell, but I suppose I'll just have to put up with it. The strange thing is, my feet are as warm as toast!'

'That's the effect of those pills I gave you. Good aren't they?'

The ice all around our campsite was very active. I think that we had all noticed that the ice noise was increasing and the terrain over which we were travelling was just a mass of broken ice, criss-crossed with large cracks. Even the larger ice-floes were just a mass of cracks. This made the choice of campsite a careful operation as it would be very easy to pitch the tent over a concealed crack, which could then open up during the night, depositing all three of us into the water while we slept, with depressing consequences.

Throughout the morning we relayed our sledges through a maze of ice ridges. The relay distances varied from only a few yards up to about half a mile or so. Steve and I would pass the time during the long walks back along the trail by pacing out the distance and comparing our separate totals.

Around midday, we were relaying the single sledge through a mass of rubble ice and small pressure ridges. All three of us were linked to the sledge in a sort of staggered fan arrangement and when we reached a spot where the ice was obviously very thin, we took a run at it. Steve was at the front and leapt over the thin ice patch, closely followed by Dave who also leapt over. Then it was my turn. I launched myself into the air, but as I did so, the sledge crashed into a block of ice which stopped it, and me, dead. My full fifteen and-a-half stones came crashing down and the thin ice stood no chance. I plunged straight through into the icy black water. My right leg was just out of the water on a floating ice block and my right hand was on the far side of the lead, but the rest of me, apart from my head, was under water. My left glove and boot filled with water and I could feel the ice cold water start to trickle into my underclothes. Automatically I started to shouting to Steve and Dave: 'Get me out! Get me out!'

They rushed back to me, but found it impossible to pull me out because the tension on my hauling line was stopping them. They had to heave the sledge closer, which would then give enough slack line for them to pull me clear of the water. The problem was that as the line came slack, I sank deeper into the water. By this time I was soaked to the skin and still shouting 'Get me out', or words to that effect, and I think that the others then realised that I wasn't enjoying the swim, so they both gave a terrific heave at my hauling harness and I was out on solid ice once more. Out of the water, my clothing froze solid within seconds in the −40°C air, and there was nothing for it but to put up the tent and change my clothes. It took the rest of the day to slowly thaw me out, and I climbed into my only spare set of Duofold thermal underwear and fleece salopettes. My unfortunate dunking had also damaged my frostbitten fingers, which by now had formed into large tender blisters and I had burst most of them in the struggle to get out of the water.

In the evening I was in intense pain from my hands, making it impossible to write up my diary. Thankfully, Steve and Dave took over the tasks of cooking, even though by now Dave had two frostbitten fingers of his own, which must have been giving him pain. Once again we could not get two-way contact with Flo, although we could hear him loud and clear. He passed messages from our families which were a great morale boost, especially after today's epic events.

All of day nine was spent in an attempt to dry out my left boot. Both stoves were revved up to full power as we tried to melt most of the encrusted ice from the boot liners. After a full day the ice had melted and the boots were hot and scorched in places, but still very damp. I knew that as soon as the stove was turned off for the night, the damp boots would freeze up solid, making them very difficult, if not impossible, to put on in the morning. I spent the night cuddling the duffle inner boots inside my sleeping bag, with the hope that they would remain soft enough to put on. The constantly low temperatures were now worrying us, with the thermometer still registering somewhere below −50°C, and we guessed closer to −60°C during the night. Lack of sleep was now affecting all of us. Our sleeping bags were now so full of ice that they were almost useless, which forced us to sleep fully clothed. I even wore a down jacket inside my sleeping bag, but still could not combat the cold. Our sleeping bags had slowly become silent killers, and we knew it.

At some point during the night, my right hand had become so cold that I received a secondary frostbite blister on top of the original injury. Steve started to prepare breakfast, and while it was cooking he told me that during the night he had become so cold that he was seriously worried about going to sleep, in case he never woke up again. At several stages through the night, I had experienced bouts of uncontrollable, violent shivering which had also worried me. It was obvious that we were very close to being overtaken by hypothermia.

The pain in my hands seemed to come in waves, gradually increasing in intensity to a level which became hard to bare, before subsiding to a dull throbbing ache. Persistently low temperatures were not helping matters. Meteorological data given to us by our Russian friends suggested that at this time of year and at this latitude, the expected daytime temperature should be around −25°C, with the lowest temperature to be expected being −40°C. This was definitely not the case. Our night-time temperature continued to be cripplingly low and only rose to −40°C during the day.

In the evening we made brief radio contact with Flo and passed over an update of the journey so far, for him to pass on to *The Guardian*. Dave also passed on the news that I had serious frostbite in my hands and that our sleeping bags were now almost useless and giving us serious cause for concern. Flo asked what our plan was and Dave replied that we would for the moment carry on in a faint hope that things might improve. After the radio was switched off, Dave looked at both Steve and I and with a big grin said, 'It could be worse. Anyway, the good news is, it's pasta for supper tonight!'

Day eleven was the first of March and due to a combination of pain, cold, ice noise and Steve's snoring, sleep had been out of the question. The exceptionally low temperatures continued to drain our reserves and twelve hours after the last meal meant that your stomach was empty and the body started to collapse. Dave lit the stove and started to cook up some food. By now my hands were finished, with even the simplest of tasks becoming impossible to carry out without causing me intense pain. At times, my fingers felt as if they were on fire and about to burst. It required all the will power I had left just to get out of my sleeping bag and put on my boots, as each time I touched something my hands were racked with pain. Added to this, there was a strong danger of infection as the blisters on my thumbs, in particular, were by now weeping open wounds.

It took a seemingly endless four hours from Dave starting breakfast to being packed and ready to move. I felt a strong sense of personal failure at being stupid enough to get injured so seriously that it could now jeopardise the entire project. We moved off and had a pretty good day's march for once, covering almost four nautical miles over heavily fractured thin ice. We relayed all day, covering all gained ground three times and only stopping twice for 'Horchoc' and 'Tweet'. Through the day the thermometer continued to read −40°C, which was far too cold for this kind of hard physical activity.

Another sleepless night took us into day twelve, with the extreme temperatures and ice-filled sleeping bags continuing to make sleep a difficult state to achieve. As we finished breakfast, the sun came up and lit up a perfect cloudless sky. On mornings like this, you can easily forget all the pain, cold, fatigue etc., with the raw beauty of the Arctic wilderness soaking into your every fibre, and regardless of all the pain and danger you would not wish to be anywhere else.

We were taking a long time to get going each morning and now

Steve was having to help me into my harness. We hauled away for the first relay leg of the day, heading into a stiff northerly breeze, which created large white patches of frostnip on our noses and cheeks in just a few seconds. We were continuously watching each other and as soon as white patches appeared we would stop and warm the area up. Putting a hand over the affected area warmed it up and was sufficient to cure the problem. Five gruelling relays later we stopped and made camp, as cloud started to gather in the southern sky. Our thermometer had yet again showed −40°C all day.

Throughout the late evening, the cloud continued to thicken. This was in fact a good sign, as we hoped that a change in the weather may just warm up the temperature a little. No such luck. The extreme cold persisted and checking the thermometer became a boring task, as the liquid stayed inside the bulb, well off the scale. Our two stoves were beginning to suffer from the effects of the continuously low temperatures. Ice blocked the valves, which meant that the stoves could not hold their pressure, priming spirit became so supercooled that it refused to light, and springs inside the non-return valves seemed to loose their 'springiness' and refused to work. We found that by adding spirit to the paraffin, it cured the ice build-up in the burner, but both stoves continued to cause problems. While trying to repair the stoves, our hands became covered in soot and paraffin and our clothes began to reek of paraffin also.

Day thirteen dawned with a cloudy sky, but without any improvement in the temperatures. Steve had developed a very sore, blistered heel which must have given him pain during the day, but he seemed to shrug it off. After another very sluggish start, we began our routine of relaying the sledges through the maze of pressure ridges, which blocked our route to the north. We were still travelling over very young first-year sea ice, with not a sign of older, thicker ice anywhere. The ice was still very active, with cracks in every direction. After each relay leg, either Dave or myself would climb to the top of the largest pressure ridge and try to pick out the easiest route. On our return from these scouting trips the other two would routinely ask the question: 'What's it

117

look like ahead?', and the ritual answer would be: 'It's . . . ing bollocks', and it usually was.

After six hours of hard relaying we stopped and made camp in the only half-decent safe spot that we could find. The tough physical labour and extreme cold was really taking its toll and our bodies were running out of fuel a lot earlier than they should, even though we were stuffing as many calories down our throats as we possibly could each day, without being sick. After the evening meal fatigue finally took hold of me, and as soon as I crawled into my now ice-filled sleeping bag I fell into a deep dreamless sleep.

The following morning I awoke feeling refreshed after catching up on lost sleep and my frostbite blisters had started to dry up, with the skin turning a dark black/brown colour. We managed to get an early start and were packed up and off along the trail by 10.00 a.m. The ice conditions showed no sign of improving, but we did come across one piece of older ice today. It was much thicker and, because of that, it floated higher out of the water than all the surrounding ice.

By now we had become pretty good at relaying, slowly trying to make each separate leg just that bit longer than the previous one. I think that we all looked forward to the return walks, as it gave us a chance to stride out without having a dead weight attached to your back. Walking back also meant that the sun was in your face. Sometimes the sun would produce spectacular solar parhelia, or 'sun dogs', produced by the sun's rays refracting through ice crystals in the upper atmosphere. While hauling the sun was always behind us, which was of benefit, as we could use our shadows as a north indicator and didn't have to keep checking our direction with a compass.

After only one and a half miles, we were stopped by open water. Dave and I searched in both directions for a suitable place to cross, but could not find one. We had come prepared with flotation tubes which could be attached to the sledges so we could cross open water, but in these temperatures it was quicker and safer to wait for the lead to freeze over.

During the evening, the pain in my hands was as bad as ever and the cold remained unbearably intense. Each night now the sleeping bags were unpacked and instead of looking like inviting, cosy cocoons, they were cold, ice-filled lumps. Their insulating properties were by that time psychological, but having no spares we had no alternative but to keep on using them. We ate our evening meal while the beacon sent out its by now usual Code 1 signal.

The coldest night yet followed, forcing an early start. At 10 a.m. we pulled away from the campsite for the first relay. Relay followed relay, until the weather closed in and forced us to make camp. We took advantage of this early stop and tried to dry out some of our clothes. With both stoves going full tilt, we hung up our gloves, socks, hats, etc., from the washing line in the top of the tent and then settled down with a mug of tea and watched them steam merrily away. When I was hauling the sledges during the day, my mind became numbed by the physical strain of each relay leg, but during enforced lie-ups like this I found my mind free to wander on to other things. Mostly on these occasions my thoughts naturally became filled with images of my wife Tracey and my young daughter Hannah. I didn't realise just how much they both meant to me and how much I had been missing them. Dave would talk about his girlfriend, Jane, and Steve would question him as to whether or not he had made his mind up to ask her to marry him. The debate would continue and many arguments for and against marriage would be discussed, with me as the only married representative acting as mediator.

Bad weather continued to plague us throughout the afternoon, with the thermometer fluid still refusing to rise out of its bulb. Our sleeping bags were just a mass of ice and weighed a ton. We toyed with the idea of taking turns to stay up through the night to keep the stove going non-stop. It would seem a sensible idea and far more acceptable than dying in our sleep from hypothermia.

It was now 6 March and at this latitude we could expect to see the start of the Arctic spring, with a slight warming in the temperatures. But it appeared not to be the case this year, and the temperature still fell to below −50°C each night. At the end of a day's march, we were totally spent. The meal eaten for breakfast had been burnt off some time ago and your body had started to use up some of its fat reserves; therefore, we were starting to lose weight.

In the evening we had a conference to decide our course of action from now on. It was clear that we were all deeply worried about the dangerous state of the sleeping bags. Should the low temperatures continue, then our survival could not be guaranteed. Then there was the state of my hands, which by now looked bloody awful. It was a long soul-searching discussion, which concluded that this extreme cold could not last much longer and milder weather must just be around the corner. We convinced ourselves that once warmer temperatures arrived, then we would feel much better and things would improve. We would carry on.

Not long after we had turned in for the night, the tent shook violently. This took us by surprise and Dave and I shot upright in our sleeping bags wondering what the hell it could be. The tent shook again, as if someone or something was pulling at the guy lines. At this Steve's sleepy head poked out of his bag and angrily said, 'Who's doing that?', obviously thinking that one of us was playing a practical joke on him. But by this time, both Dave and I seriously suspected that it could only be a polar bear. I reached down the side of the tent and took the .357 handgun out of its holster. The other gun was outside on Dave's sledge. I cocked the hammer on the gun, which caused intense pain in my fingers and my skin stuck to the supercool metal. But at that moment I had too many other thoughts on my mind for the pain to worry me much. Dave knelt by the tent doorway and at the count of three he unzipped the door. I poked my head outside into the icy blast and quickly shone my headtorch into the gloom and, to my horror, two bright sparkling eyes reflected back the light. I aimed the gun, but then the animal moved briefly into my light and I could see not one but two pure white Arctic foxes. They were also the biggest I have ever seen. Compared with foxes I have seen in the Canadian Arctic, these were at least twice their size. We knew that foxes ranged all over the Arctic ocean, but being scavengers by nature, their usual tactic was to follow polar bears around, cleaning up any leftovers. The two foxes stared back at me for a split second before disappearing into the Arctic night.

We relaxed back into our sleeping bags and spent some time joking about thinking the foxes were a bear. It had certainly given us a fright, but also it had been the only sign of life we had seen in sixteen days. Steve had by this time returned to his favourite state and was snoring at full volume.

The following morning I awoke cold and aching after an uncomfortable night, but the day looked like it was going to be a good one, so we packed up and made an early start. More and more monotonous relays through a very active region. Temperatures still cripplingly low and draining all three of us. If only the temperature would rise to around −30°C it would make a world of difference.

My hands gave me trouble all day, with constant pain. I asked Steve for a painkiller which helped a little, but I knew that as long as I subjected my hands to the extreme cold, their condition was only going to deteriorate. I constantly cursed myself for being so stupid, and it now looked like it would affect the outcome of the expedition.

On day eighteen, I had reached a point where I could almost overcome the pain by a force of will. I could quite successfully shut off the pain and started to do more and more without the help of the others. The quicker we got going in the mornings, the sooner we would warm up and thaw out our bones which helped to make you feel better. Once on the go, the days were full of wild beauty, which somehow seemed to make all the pain and suffering strangely worthwhile. However, the nights were absolute purgatory, because as you tried to sleep, your pain control stopped and the pain returned with a vengeance, waking you up.

After breakfast, Dave went outside and stamped around swinging his arms about, trying to coax a small amount of circulation into his feet and hands, The temperature still hovered around −50°C, making the simple task of loading the sledges a long slow job. We had jointly decided to lighten our loads by discarding two of our three sets of flotation tubes, along with three of our sledge bags. We all had very mixed feelings about this line of action purely on environmental grounds, but now circumstances had reduced our reasoning to a basic sense of survival and this sort of measure had to be taken and thus became acceptable. Lighter sledges would give us the chance of making better mileage each day and would be less punishing to haul. Relay followed monotonous relay, until by midday we had completed four very long relay legs and stopped for a well deserved rest and a drink of 'Horchoc'. The warming effect of this drink seemed to cancel out the chilling cold caused by your sweat cooling and freezing against your skin and in between the layers of your clothing.

By the time we pitched our tent, we had slogged out eight long relays and were very pleased with our day. This was our best day yet, but if the temperatures continued to refuse to rise and give us a chance to recover at night, we wouldn't be able to keep up this heavy work load for very much longer. But, with a combination of ice-filled sleeping bags and exceptionally low temperatures, we were lucky just to survive through the nights at all.

During the night the sky clouded over and the thermometer slowly rose up the scale, coming to rest at the −30°C mark. It would appear that all our prayers had been answered and we packed up for an early start. The twenty-degree rise in temperature was really noticeable and the day felt positively 'balmy'. Hauling away from the campsite for our first leg of the day, we all had a strong feeling of optimism and hoped that our luck had changed and this was the start of better conditions to come.

As was now our usual routine, we set off with one sledge, hauled it as far as possible, then walked back along the trail for the other two. Repeating this over and over again, we slowly moved northwards, but as we moved we noticed that we were moving into a very active area, with more cracks and more open water than ever before. Eventually, we found ourselves hemmed in among large pressure ridges and were forced to camp on a small pan of ice, which had a lead of open water running along its northern edge about thirty feet from our tent.

All through the evening and into the night the ice noise increased, with some noises sounding like distant canon fire, while others were much louder and closer to our tent. A couple of hours after turning in, the ice floe on which we were camped gave a violent lurch, which was followed by a loud bang. It felt like the whole thing had tilted, then settled back down into the water. Even Steve sat up in his sleeping bag with a worried look on his face. It was obvious that ice pressure was building up and something would have to give sooner or later. We just hoped and prayed that it would not be our ice floe which had to give. After a while the ice noise seemed to subside and we all settled back down and tried to sleep.

The following morning dawned fine with crystal-clear skies. This was good for travelling, but it also meant that the temperature had once more plummeted back down to around −45°C, and our brief respite from the debilitating effects of extreme cold was over. We decided to get off early, as it was better to be up and on the move rather than festering inside frozen sleeping bags. Dave and I went outside while Steve packed up the pots and stove. Dave jogged around trying to get warm, when he suddenly shouted out, 'Bloody hell, come and have a look.' I went over to where he was standing and could see that our ice floe had split in half during the night. This explained the loud bang last night. A crack about five feet wide had opened up about twenty feet from the tent to our east, with frost smoke gently rising from the now exposed inky black water. We left the campsite as quickly as we could, detemined to try and get clear of this region as soon as possible.

To our relief, after about three hours of hauling, we started to move out on to larger ice floes and slowly increased the distance of each progressive relay leg, until by the end of the day we estimated that we must have moved our sledges about five miles further north.

As we were camping up for the night, the sun sank below the horizon and as it did I felt the temperature sink also. All day the thermometer had read −40°C and now it was falling again. After our evening meal and to our total amazement, we made our best contact with Flo in Aberdeen yet. In fact, so good were the two-way communications that Dave decided to take advantage of this unique opportunity and asked Flo to telephone his girlfriend Jane in Cumbria so he could talk to her. This proved to be a great success and calls to my wife Tracey and Steve's folks followed. We all passed on our love and thoughts to them all, and after the radio link-up was over we sat and talked about our separate families for quite some time and wondered how they must have felt being dragged out of bed so early in the morning to answer a telephone call from three madmen floating in a tent out on the Arctic Ocean!

A very cold night followed with no sleep at all and my frostbitten hands giving me Hell. Day twenty-one dawned clear yet again and we prepared for a hard, cold day. We were now moving through an area of quite large ice floes, which helped by allowing us to make longer relays over some good ice. However, the daytime temperature still remained far too low and relentlessly sapped the life out of us. It was obvious that we would not be able to put up with it very much longer. Having to move forward in relays has slowed down our progress north drastically and we were all in agreement, that at this rate we stood little chance of completing our original plan. Our sleeping bags were trying to kill us each night and are increasing in weight daily. We dreaded the thought of getting into them each night and night-time became an eight-hour fight for life. Just to survive through the night without being snuffed out by the cold, was a miracle in itself.

On day twenty-two, we awoke to find that the wind had veered round from the north to the south, blowing at about ten knots. We now had another chance to use our parawings and maybe increase our daily mileage, so we packed up for an early start.

Conditions were more or less perfect for the parawings, and after rearranging the sledge loads into three equal loads, we set off under sail power. We were now in a region of large ice floes, with only low pressure ridges dividing them. The ice surface was pretty smooth, and once we got going I simply jogged along by the side of the sledge, allowing the parawing to do all the work. I found this form of travel very exhilarating and it also kept you very warm. We took full advantage of our good fortune and sledged all day, making the wind do as much work as possible, until fading light and bad ice conditions forced us to stop. We were in better spirits after a long day which had put another five miles behind us, and with a southerly wind blowing we may even end up drifting a few miles north during the night.

Another long, cold, sleepless night followed and I really didn't think we could carry on much longer. I was sure that the others felt the same, but we didn't mention it. It had been a combination of uncontrollable events which had brought us to this point, starting with bad ice conditions at the very beginning of the expedition when our loads were at their heaviest, then the slow failure of our sleeping bags and my frostbite injuries. All this in cripplingly low temperatures had now placed the whole team in a serious situation. The risk of being overcome by hypothermia during the night had become a very real danger and a constant worry. Ironically, most expeditions run into trouble due to lack of food and fuel, but here we were loaded up to the gunwales with enough supplies and fuel to stay out on the ice for a further seventy-seven days. We were on a diet of 6,050 calories per day each, but our bodies were still collapsing under the severe conditions and we were losing weight. There was nothing much for it but to pack up and move north, each of us knowing full well the danger which we were now in. We were also aware that even if we called for the expedition to be removed from the ice, the danger would not be instantly over as it could take several days to organise an aircraft and for it to reach our position out on the ice. Between now and then, we would have to try and remain alive.

After only two miles or so, we came across a freshly frozen lead, which headed in a roughly northerly direction, so we dropped down off the ice floe onto the new ice and followed it along. Hauling the sledges on smooth new ice is very easy. You can almost pull standing up straight, instead of the usual leaning forward position. Halfway along the lead we came across the first sign of seal activity since landing on the ice over three weeks ago, a small breathing hole in the thin new ice, and it was clear that the seal had only recently been there as the ice around the hole was still wet. By the end of the day we were all totally spent and close to the limits of our endurance.

Yet another bitterly cold night followed, with no let-up in the cruel temperatures. Little sleep, just short painful catnaps punctuated by bouts of uncontrollable shivering. My hands are a total mess, six blackened fingers and two black thumbs which had now started to ooze with stinking pus. To stay out on the ice in those conditions much longer would almost certainly mean the loss of some digits.

None of us wished to conclude the expedition, although we knew we were now in a seriously dangerous situation. Following breakfast, we packed up the sledges and in silence hauled away. We continued to relay for a while until we came across another freshly frozen lead. This one headed slightly west of north, so we again dropped down on to the smooth new ice and, pulling single sledges, marched in single file along this smooth Arctic motorway. As we hauled along the lead, the ice creaked and groaned, not because of our weight but due to pressure from the surrounding ice.

After only about a hundred yards, the lead closed up and forced us up onto the ice floes once more. Because I was the biggest of the three of us, I found that I could pull a single sledge over the ice floe reasonably well, and so I suggested to Steve and Dave that I thought it would be a good idea to lighten up the sledges even further by throwing away food and fuel, change our plan and go for the Pole only. With lighter sledges, we could move much faster and may just be in with a chance. I knew as I was explaining my plan that in our present physical state it was out of the question. Unfortunately, my suggestion created the spark that flashed the powder keg. Uncharacteristically, and more than likely due to the strain and exposure, both Dave and Steve exploded at me in temper. I am sure that it was not meant with any personal malice, but more as a release of tension and anger which we all felt at our sheer bad luck. Up to this point, I had always agreed to continue the journey, even though the pain in my hands had been at times unbearable, but now I knew that it was over. We were not in a position to complete our journey, and if I wanted to save my fingers from amputation I needed to get out of those conditions, and fast.

RUSSIAN ROULETTE

'Your money, or your life!'

T he tent was pitched for what we all knew would be the last time and a brew made, which we liberally laced with the last of our brandy. We knew that now was the time to call for a removal from the ice, if we were to survive at all. While the evening meal cooked, Dave tuned in the radio and fortunately made contact with Flo, albeit a faint one. Dave then passed over our request for an urgent removal from the ice. Our final GPS position fix put us at 78°14′N, 160°58′E, only one degree of latitude north of our starting position three and a half weeks ago.

Sitting in the tent, I felt a great sadness at being a cause of the end to the hopes, dreams and ambitions of all three of us. We had worked so hard together to get the expedition up and running and had struggled to the very limit of human endurance out on the ice in a determined attempt to complete our plan. But the cards were stacked against us all the way. In my mind I analysed the problems over and over again: if only the vapour barrier bags had worked, if only the temperatures had been kinder, if only I had taken more care of my hands. If only . . . if only . . . One good piece of luck was that the weather was good for flying, which gave us hope for a speedy rescue.

We had now been out on the ice for twenty-five days and still the temperature remained at −40°C throughout the night, and at 4.20 a.m. I could stand no more and lit the stove to make a brew of tea. Steve was as usual fast asleep, but Dave was awake and I passed him a mug. At 6.00 a.m. Dave tuned in the radio and spoke again to Flo, who said that the Russians would attempt to fly out to our position tomorrow. We then had to wait out the day until the evening radio schedule, before we could get a further update. Steve produced a letter which he handed to me; on the front was written, 'Not to be opened until at the North Pole'. I instantly recognised the handwriting as Tracey's and just burst into tears. My emotions exploded and I realised just how much I had missed her as I read the letter and certainly didn't feel like the perfect husband and father. All I wished for now was to see her as soon as possible. Frustratingly, we could not make contact with Flo on the evening schedule, so we turned in for another miserable, painful night.

Day twenty-six dawned after one of the most wretched and painful nights of my entire life. Yet again the thermometer liquid had shrunk back into its bulb and had been reading off the scale all night. We had good news from Flo on our early morning radio schedule, who informed us that the pilots based in Chokurdakh were happy to effect our rescue, but there was a catch. The pilots had increased their charter price by a factor of three and were basically saying that's our price, take it, or they will just simply leave us to die out on the ice. This, I thought, was a very sick form of Russian blackmail and an attitude which I had somehow come to expect based on all our previous dealings with them. We obviously could not meet their extortionate demands, so Flo suggested that he would get in contact with Dmitry Shparo in Moscow and request that he try and find a more affordable alternative, but this would take a little time.

Dmitry could take all the time he wished, as now the weather had changed for the worse. Thick cloud had built up and a strong northerly wind was now blowing. Surface spindrift caused by the wind was completely obliterating all surface features on the ice, making the landing of an aircraft impossible. Our situation was now becoming serious. We were unsure if a suitable arrangement could ever be made with the Aeroflot pilots, who were obviously not bothered one way or the other about our plight. It was now a simple matter of will power, to try and survive long enough for a rescue flight to be organised. We had ample food and fuel, so we started to keep both stoves going all the time. We drifted into a sleepy routine of dozing, then reading, then eating, then dozing again. The stoves were by now in a poor state and required constant attention to keep them working. When they ran out of fuel, we took turns to fill them up. The inside of our tent was by now becoming encrusted with a thick layer of ice, which was being stained grey by the soot being given off by our ailing stoves. Luckily, good contact was made with Flo, who passed a list of changes to our SARSAT/COSPAS beacon codes, just in case we lost radio communications over the next few critical days.

We had drifted into a state of limbo, with only one task on our minds: to survive long enough to be picked up by the Russian rescue aircraft. It was far too dangerous to go to sleep leaving the stoves burning, but we needed the heat to survive as our sleeping bags were useless. Eventually, we decided to stay awake in turns through the night and keep the stoves going. The 'nightwatchman' would then be able to catch up on sleep during the daytime. In fact this worked out very well, as the Five Nations rugby tournament was on at the time and it gave us the opportunity to tune in on the radio and follow its progress. The SARSAT/COSPAS beacon was activated, this time with a new Code 4, which indicated to Flo that the weather at our position was poor for flying.

By the morning of day twenty-eight our stoves had started to give continuous trouble, especially the Whisperlite which was spluttering out sooty fumes all the time. Should this stove give out altogether, that would only leave the Optimus Loke stove to keep us alive, and even this was starting to give more trouble. Should both stoves pack up, our life expectancy would be very short indeed. One-way contact was made with Flo on the evening schedule, who said that he had contacted Dmitry and that he had made arrangements with the pilots in Chersky settlement for a rescue flight. The pilots would fly out to our position as soon as he gave them the go-ahead. They intended to use two An-2 planes, with a helicopter standing by on the Siberian coast just in case. For this rescue work, they were asking for a fee of $30,000 US. Flo then explained that the terms were that Dmitry would only give the go-ahead when he had received confirmation that the money had been deposited into his own personal bank account which, wait for it, was held in Vienna! We were at his mercy and had no choice but to accept his terms. We either paid up the money and possibly survived, or stayed out on the ice . . . permanently.

Things were not looking good. We had just enough money to pay for the rescue flight, but it would take even more time to make the bank transfers before the flights could be made. We explained to Flo that our situation was now very precarious and we would very much appreciate some urgency from the Russian pilots. The weather was now improving at our end at least and flying was now possible, but the Russians only had one chance, and if they failed to reach us, we could not afford a second attempt. We activated the beacon and transmitted a Code 3, which indicated to Flo that the weather had improved and was good for flying at our end.

Dave made contact with Flo at 6 a.m. on the morning of day twenty-nine. Flo told us that he had received our beacon transmission and had relayed the information to Russia. He had also transferred the money to Vienna and faxed a copy of the bank transfer to Dmitry so that he could now give the go-ahead for the rescue flights. If everything was OK, the Chersky pilots were planning to take off from Chersky at 6 a.m. the following morning, which would put them overhead of our position at around 1 p.m. in the afternoon. Another schedule was then agreed for the evening and we started to prepare our equipment for a quick getaway.

Throughout the day and into the evening, the weather remained clear and settled. Our beacon continued to pump out its Code 3 signal and we prayed to God that the clear weather would hold. We spent the night awake, listening to the BBC World Service, eating up our stock of chocolate and drinking soup and tea.

It was now our thirtieth day afloat on this thin scum of moving, broken ice and we were all hoping that it would be our last. Mercifully, the morning dawned fine, clear and sunny, which gave us a good chance of being airlifted back to land. We just had to hope that the weather in Chersky was the same. Flo came up on the radio, and although we could not speak to him he gave us the welcome news that the aircraft had in fact taken off and was on track for our position. He then asked if at local noon we would activate one of our personal emergency beacons to assist the aircraft to locate us, and also to find something to burn which would produce plenty of smoke. This would give a good indication of surface wind strength and direction to the pilots when they approached to land on the ice.

For the rest of the morning we kept our fingers crossed that all would go well and packed up our gear in readiness for the plane's arrival. I took a nylon sledge bag out on to the ice and filled it with some of our now surplus food, which I then soaked liberally with paraffin. This would make lots of smoke, I thought. Back inside the tent, I took a GPS position fix, which now put us at 77°58'N, 161°13'E. While we had been waiting for our rescue plans to be sorted out, we had drifted over sixteen nautical miles to the south-east, that's just a little over three miles per day.

Steve served up a brew of tea and we sat and talked over the events of the last six weeks. We were beaten, we accepted that, but we all felt that we had let a hell of a lot of people down. People that had supported us and had strong faith in our abilities to succeed. From a personal point of view, I felt that all three of us had given our all to the project and I would challenge anyone to do better than us, given the same set of circumstances. My two companions never failed to impress me, with their total commitment and unselfish determination to give of their best. Steve reached over and took hold of my right hand, which by now was really smelly and infected: 'Let's take a look at yer fingers, mate,' and after a short examination he said, 'Yes, we will have to sort them out as soon as we get to Chersky, and I think it's got to be a course of the old ABs (antibiotics) for you my old son.'

At local noon precisely, Steve pulled the pin on one of our personal rescue beacons and stood it on the roof of the tent and we packed up everything apart from the tent and Loke stove, which we kept running to keep us alive while we waited. To pass the time we either sat inside the tent and talked, or jogged around on the ice to keep warm. I used these last few hours to absorb as much of the desolation of my surroundings as possible. Our lonely little tent was surrounded by one of the Earth's finest examples

131

of nature just doing its own thing. The sheer size and power of the Arctic drift ice sends you into a sort of sensory overload. To the south, the sun's cool disc is floating above the horizon and lighting up an almost cloudless sky. It's hard to face the fact that the sun is just a huge nuclear bomb which is slowly burning out and flooding the Earth with its heat and light. The light was quite brilliant, but as for the heat, well, not much of that was filtering through the atmosphere onto this remote place.

We were about to leave the Arctic ocean under very much different circumstances than any of us would have wished, but that is the way the cards were dealt to us and we were certain that we could not have played our hand any better. But, was an unsupported crossing of the Arctic ocean at all possible? Had we just bitten off more than we could chew? Well, in theory the crossing is possible, but the expedition would also have to have a huge amount of good fortune, and this is out of your control. No matter how much experience the team has, or how well prepared the expedition is, the Arctic can stop you.

Right on time, the sound of aircraft engines could be heard. Dave came running out of the tent with a blazing piece of paper in his hand, which he threw on to the paraffin-soaked food bag. There was a 'whoosh' and the whole bag burst into flames. By now the two tiny planes were almost overhead, and it started to appear that they had not seen us. Both aircraft then veered off and headed to our west, even though we had our beacon switched on and the food bag was by now belching out a long trail of grey/black smoke.

Steve made all attempts to speak to the aircraft using the speech mode of our SARBE beacon, but it soon became obvious that none of the aircrew could speak English, and as Steve spoke little Russian it all seemed pointless. Then, just as we all thought that that was the end, the lead aircraft suddenly banked over and started to head back towards our position. The small An-2 swooped down overhead and had obviously seen us. It was then only a few minutes before the plane gently touched down on to the ice and taxied over to our tent; the second followed a minute later.

The crew of both planes climbed out on to the ice and greeted us with great gusto, and not knowing that my hands were severely frostbitten grabbed hold of them and shook them violently which brought tears to my eyes. One of the reasons why the aircraft had not initially spotted us was that they had been told to look out for a 'red'-coloured tent, and of course ours was in fact blue. Before long the sledges were loaded on to the aircraft and strapped down for the flight back to land. The Russians didn't seem to be in any rush to leave as it was such a fine day. They walked around taking photographs and helped themselves to our spare food packs and fuel bottles. I was very grateful to one of the crew, who gave me a dry pair of fur mitts, which he had warmed up for me. With the combination of warm mitts and another painkiller from Steve, I settled down in one of the planes for the journey back to Chersky and we each said our goodbyes to the ice, which had been our home for so long. It all seemed dreamlike, that this is not the way it should be happening and what went wrong? If we can believe in fate, then it was obvious that we were not meant to succeed this time.

The take-off was smooth and gentle, and once in the air the planes circled around giving us a good view to the north. It looked horrific, with large areas of open water and high pressure ridges for as far as the eye could see, which from this position was a hell of a long way. Had things been different and we were still in a position to be travelling, then the ice conditions up ahead would almost certainly have stopped us in any event. Flying south, the change in the ice conditions was dramatic. Vast areas of open water and fresh ice now occupied our outward route.

We all felt depressed in the knowledge that the expedition failed to reach its goal and that we had let many people down, but in fact the opposite is often the case, that by having the determination and guts to even dream of attempting a project such as ours, we actually inspired many people of all ages. On my return to Britain I had a flood of letters, all of which confirmed this, and one letter in particular, written by a teacher from Middlesex, I think said it all:

Dear Stephen, David and Clive,

I have just read the latest article about your recent expedition in today's Education *Guardian*. Having read Stephen's comment about feeling that you have disappointed the schoolchildren who have been following your progress, I felt I must write and tell you about the effect that your endeavours have had on my class.

I am an English teacher at a local comprehensive. I have a low-ability class of thirty Year 8 children (12–13 year olds). As part of a diary/journal writing project, I read them your weekly reports. They are a noisy class with poor concentration skills, but they sat and listened with interest each week. The week I read about the 'fourth person' phenomenon, we were able to have an orderly discussion with pupils asking questions and listening to each other – a real one-off breakthrough for that class.

I don't have the article in front of me to quote the exact words, but my class wholeheartedly agreed that survival and safe return cannot be deemed failure.

Thank you for inspiring my class.

Best wishes to you all.

POSTSCRIPT

'The breath of God produces ice,
  and the broad waters become frozen.
He loads the clouds with moisture;
  he scatters his lightning through them.
At his direction they swirl around
  over the face of the whole earth
  to do whatever he commands them.
He brings the clouds to punish men,
  or to favour them and show his love.'
– Job, 37:10–13

As I sit at my desk, putting the finishing touches to this book, the tips of my fingers and the tips of my toes are still numb and occasionally give me pain. So was it all worth it? – Yes. It is a fact that most adventurers suffer from a severe form of short-term memory loss. Although I find it a relatively simple task to remember events and write them down, the pain and suffering has now been filed away permanently in the deep recesses of my mind and forgotten, with plans for future adventures now taking their place. At times during expeditions, you often wish that you could be back in the warmth of your home and in the arms of your loved ones. But, once at home, the strange attraction takes hold of your very soul once more and all you wish for is to be back on the ice again.

Over the years, I have built up a deep and lasting love of wild places, whether it be mountains, moorland, or polar wastelands. So strong is my love of these regions of the world that I will always be drawn toward them. I am a willing sufferer of Robert Peary's so called 'polar fever', and I sincerely hope that I am never cured.

135

ACKNOWLEDGEMENTS

While some sponsors and supporters have been mentioned in the text of this book, I am indebted to the following companies and individuals whose help, support and encouragement has been overwhelming. I apologise to anyone who I have inadvertently missed.

ORGANISATIONS

Littlewoods	Finance
Carlsberg–Tetley	Sledge sponsors
Bass Brewery	Finance
Greenhall Group plc	Finance and advice
Royal Geographical Society	Approval and grant
Morson International	Finance
Nirex	Finance
H & L Electrical Ltd	Finance
Paul Dinsdale Associates	Finance
The Guardian	Finance, publicity, educational project, film
Glaxo	Finance
Syntex Pharmaceuticals	Finance
Astra Pharmaceuticals	Finance
Rank Xerox	Photocopying
Duplication Express	PR Videos
Agrofil Ltd	Dried food
BNFL	Photocopying
Bridgdale	Socks
British Airways	All flights and cargo transport
Duofold	Thermal clothing

Acknowledgements

Highland guides — Skis & equipment
Input — Nutrition information
Mintlaw Radio — Radio/beacons etc.
Nikwax Paramo — Shell clothing
On-line — Fax switch
Optimus International — Stove and spares, Sigg bottles
Parawing — Parawings
Rab Down Equipment — Sleeping bags, down boots & jackets

Rolex watch company — Rolex award, PR support
Snowsled Ltd — Sledges & hauling harnesses
Wild Country — Gloves & overboots
Karrimor International Ltd — Sleeping bags & foam mats
Khyam Designs — Tents
Lyon Equipment — Headtorch
Silva UK Ltd — Compasses
Jack Wolfskin — Rucksacks, waterproof bags, fleece jackets, trousers, stuff sacks, gloves, shirts, balaclavas

Barn Door Shop, Wasdale — Misc. kit
Derbyshire Constabulary — Firearms advice
Ken Bancroft — Firearms
Typhoo Tea, Premier Brands — Instant tea
Damart — Thermal clothing
H.A. West X-Ray Ltd — Loan of cameras
Fuji UK — Film
Colorcraft — Film processing
Kaufman Footwear — Mukluks
Bradley Air Services — Flights
Coleman — Stainless steel flasks, pressure lantern

SCA Packaging — Packing cases
Lloyds Packaging — Freight packaging
Altitude — Waterproof bags
Mercury Communications — Video conferencing
Manning, Salvage & Lee — PR
Nestlé UK — Chocolate
Image Design & Print — Photocopying
Trans Euro — Freight Transport
Magellan Instruments — Satellite navigation equipment
Alpinex International — Undersuits
The Alpenstock — Stove etc
The Adventure Club, Moscow — Logistics

Saft	Batteries
Medik CI Ltd	Space Bags
Royal Canadian Mounted Police	Advice
South Midland Communications	Radio equipment
Woolsery Electronics	Batteries
Jotron Electronics	Beacon
The MoD	Permission to use radio frequencies
Safeway	Foodstuffs

INDIVIDUALS IN THE UK

David Baines
Wolf Beringers
David Brayshaw
Susannah Brook
Keith Burgess
Duncan Burman
Rab Carrington
Richard Chambers
Oliver Cooper
Jim Crosbie
Simon Dansie
Rodger Daynes
Paul Dinsdale
His Grace the Duke of Devonshire MC PC
Jane Falstead
Christine Fen
Caroline Ferminger
Sir Ranulph Fiennes
Sheila Fitsymons
Sir Vivian Fuchs FRS
Gil Greenhall
The Hon. Peter Greenhall
Gary Grey
Brian Hambleton
Elide Hodgson
Mr Horgan
Laurence Howell
Morag Howell
Jackie Ive
Andrew Johnston
Lisa Jones-Taylor

Acknowledgements

Rudy S. Keller
Helen Lawrenson
Dr Richard Laws CBE FRS
Vitali A. Loukiantsev (Russian Consulate, London)
Brian Markey
Carol Marshall
John Martin
Ged Mason
Sian Mitchell
Katrina Morrissy
Richard Oliver
Jenny Peacock
Tim Radford
Chief Inspector Peter Ramsbottom
Tim Roberts
Jillian Rowan-Wilde
Kay Schofield
Michael Scott
Alastair Simpson
Dr Mike Stroud
Harry Thomas
Brian Thompson
Dennis Thorpe
Sir Crispin Tickell GCMG KCVO
Tony Wale
Anne Ward
Nigel Winsor
Ian Wright
All at Save the Children

IN RUSSIA
'Alexsis' the chief pilot.
'Sergey'
'Major Sergey' our liaison officer in Tiksi.
Dmitry Shparo.
Alexander 'Sasha' Shumilov.
All the staff at the Adventure Club, Moscow.
The staff of the British Airways office, Moscow, who were marvellous.

Finally, can I give special thanks to the Chief of 'Tiksi III' for allowing us to survive his very unusual form of Siberian hospitality.

SELECTED BIBLIOGRAPHY

Abruzzi, Duke of, *On the Polar Star*, 2 vols (London, Hutchinson, 1903)

Adams-Ray, Edward, *The Andrée Diaries* (London, John Lane & Bodley Head Ltd 1931)

Bain, Arther, *Life & Explorations of Fridtjof Nansen* (London, Walter Scott Ltd, 1897)

Black, John, *Nansen and the Frozen North* (London, George Routledge & Sons Ltd, 1901)

Brogger, W.C. & Rolfsen, Nordahal, *Fridtjof Nansen, 1861–1893* (London, Longmans, Green & Co. 1896)

Brontman, L., *On the Top of the World – The Soviet expedition to the North Pole, 1937* (London, Victor Gollancz Ltd, 1938)

Bryce, George, *The Siege and Conquest of the North Pole* (London, Gibbings, 1910)

De Long, George W., *Voyage of the* Jeannette (Boston, Houghton Mifflin, 1884)

Herbert, Wally, *Across the Top of the World* (London, Longman, 1969); *The Noose of Laurels* (London, Hodder & Stoughton, 1989)

Hoehling, A.A., Jeannette *Expedition* (London, Abelard, 1967)

Johansen, Hjalmar, *With Nansen in the North* (London, Ward Lock & Co. Ltd, 1899)

Judd, Alfred, *The Conquest of the Poles* (London, T.C. & E.C. Jack Ltd, 1925)

Kuralt, Charles, *To the Top of the World* (NY, Holt, 1968)

McKinlay, William Laird, *Karluk* (Book Club Associates, 1976)

Nansen, Fridtjof, *Farthest North*, 2 vols. (NY, Harper, 1897; London, Newnes, 1898; Chatto, 1955); *The First Crossing of Greenland*, 2 vols. (London, Longmans, 1890)

Schley, Winfield, *The Rescue of Greely* (NY, Scribner, 1885)

Shackleton, Edward, *Arctic Journeys* (London, Hodder & Stoughton, 1934)

Selected Bibliography

Stefansson, Vilhjalmur, *Ultima Thule* (London, George G. Harrop & Co. 1942)

Steger, Will, *North to the Pole* (NY Times Books, 1987)

Sverdrup, Otto, *New Land*, (Longman, 1904)

Victor, Paul-Emile, *Man and Conquest of the Poles* (Simon & Schuster, 1963)

Weems, John Edward, *Peary the Explorer and the Man* (London, Eyre & Spottiswoode, 1967)

INDEX

Notes: 1. Clive Johnson is denoted C.J.   2. Trans-polar Drift Stream Expedition is denoted TPDSE

Index

Please remember that this is a library book, and that it belongs only temporarily to each person who uses it. Be considerate. Do not write in this, or any, library book.

DATE DUE

WITHDRAWN